Paper Engineering: The Basics

Structures that move, pull out, swirl and extend are a delight. A person of any age can't help but smile at a pop-up book.

When I was a kid, pop-ups were the books that I treasured, reading them over and over again, pulling tabs and spinning wheels. As an adult, the kid in me still loves those magical structures. We can use them in books in very sophisticated ways. When someone looks at one on my bookshelf, I always know when they hit one of the mechanical engineered or pop-up structures when I hear the ooohh.

These structures are crowd pleasers, but take a bit of preplanning. I suggest you enlarge most template patterns 200% or larger.

Make a mock-up little book, see instructions below. A visual example is worth its weight in gold and doing this before you try pop-ups in a book will make the transition easy.

See page 5 for instructions

Some Tips:

- Use a very strong double-stick tape for sticking these pop-ups in your book. It makes life easier.
- You can enlarge the templates at any rate to make the pop-ups fit your book. You can also make templates based on the shape of the element you want to use for most structures.
- There are some very effective pop-ups that are easy. Complicated is not always the best.
- Back all pop-ups with cardstock. You need the strength in the structure.

CUT-OUTS ON TENT

CENTER TENT

PARALLEL FOLD

Pop-Ups... Making a Mock-up

Try each pop-up first before you start doing them in an altered book. Take an hour to just use the pattern provided to make a mock-up booklet. When you continue to do these structures, you will have a hands-on example to refer to.

MATERIALS: Book binder's needle or tapestry needle • Button thread • 3 pieces of gold cardstock • Awl • Bone folder

Make a booklet - 1. Fold and score 3 gold pages in half. **2.** With the awl make three even holes in the fold of the papers. **3.** Pull your needle through the middle hole from outside the booklet into the spine and leave a tail about 3 inches long that hangs inside your booklet. Go to the top hole and pull the needle through that hole from the spine to the outside. Go past the middle hole all the way to the bottom hole and go through that hole from the outside to the inside. Go through the middle hole again and tie the two ends.

Add mock-ups - Copy templates and glue in mock-ups following directions. Be sure to make notes to yourself as you work.

Pop-Ups... Parallel Folds

The parallel fold is the easiest pop-up, and it can look very artsy. Think about what you want your audience to find and make sure a bit shows so they know to lift the flap.

Design Considerations:

This fold can be done anywhere on the book page and doesn't need to be placed over the spine of the book. It is glued on top of the page so the page itself isn't cut. The fold needs to be lifted.

Cut a rectangle of any size out of cardstock, or use a pre-scored card or file folder. If the cardstock isn't scored and folded, go ahead and do that. **1.** Cut two parallel lines from the fold into the card. 1"- 2" is large enough. **2.** Fold the tab back and forth to score it. **3.** Open the card and push the tab into the middle of the card with your finger. **4.** Glue image on tab or table (upper part of tab). **5.** Glue the card into your book. It can be placed anywhere on the page.

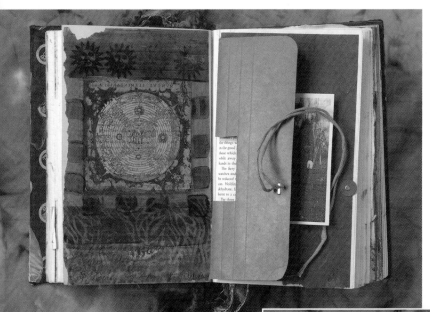

Vern and Ruth   by Beth Cote

MATERIALS: Old photo mounted on cardstock for strength • Brown Cardstock or old file folder • Collage materials

1. Cut a rectangle of any size out of cardstock or use a pre-scored card or file folder. **2.** If the cardstock isn't scored and folded, go ahead and do that. **3.** Make two parallel cuts with your scissors from the fold. The deeper you make this cut, the longer your tab or table the photo or any other item will be glued to. A cut of 1"- 2" is usually sufficient. Do not make a cut longer than the half point on your cardstock. **4.** Fold this back and forth several times. **5.** Open the card and with your finger push the tab through the opening into the middle of the card. This is the table. **6.** Glue the photo to the table lengthwise. **7.** Glue the card into the book and collage around it.

Tip:
You can do a lot of variations with the Parallel Fold.

Make many tables and glue a letter to each fold, glue a tag on your fold, or a unique shape.

The possibilities are endless.

ALL SIX DOORS OPEN
See page 3 for a larger photo

DETAIL OF ONE POP-UP DOOR

Pop-Ups... Advanced Parallel Folds

Wrapping paper is used for the delicate butterfly and dragonfly pop-ups in this altered calendar. Look around you with new eyes for collage materials. You will be surprised at what you will find.

Flower Book

by Joyce Yuen

MATERIALS: Wrapping paper or stamps that are symmetrical • Cardstock • Alphabet from the book/CD Decorated Initials (*Shambhala Publications*, ISBN 1-57062-483-6) • Velcro • Gel pens

1. Print alphabets on cardstock. Cut out leaving 1/4" sides for hinges or border. Score and fold about 1/4" from the side. **2.** Glue cardstock hinge onto the book page. Cut out images from various gift wraps. Leave 1/4" on the left and right side, score and fold to form hinges. **3.** Score the center of images and cut around the focal point making sure you leave some of the edges attached to the border. **4.** Fold images in half, then pull the focal point up to form a Mountain Fold. Glue one hinge of an image to cardstock. Adjust and check position of the images, then put glue on the other side of hinge.

5. Close the flap and glue to the book page. Continue to glue the remaining images to cardstock and book page.

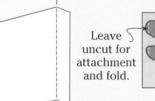

1. Cut outer piece. Valley Fold a crease for hinge.

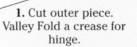

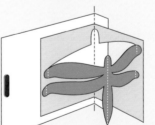

Valley Fold
Valley Fold

Mountain Fold

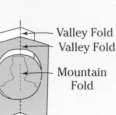

Leave uncut for attachment and fold.

Do not cut.

2. Cut out inside Pop-Up image. Leave a little of the image uncut for a hinge. Valley Fold at wings and Mountain Fold at center back.

3. Glue Pop-Up image to outer piece at fold. Add Velcro.

4. Cut Out a circle shape. Try different shapes or images.

1. Fold image in half with a Mountain Fold, so the image itself is on the outside of the fold.

2. Cut around image, leaving the widest part of the image still attached to the paper.

3. Make Valley Folds on the wing parts that are still attached to the paper. **4.** Push the body of the butterfly outwards with your finger.

Flash of Memory   by Joyce Yuen

STAMP CREDITS: *Stampers Anonymous* Alphabet •
Paula Best Large Wings • *Limited Edition* Small wings
• *Rubbermoon* small row of dolls • *Fringe Elements -
Claudine Hellmuth* Child w/wings • *Adorned Surface,
Stamp Out Cute, Fusion Art, Rubbermoon* Dolls •
Claudine Hellmuth alphabet game tiles • *Ancient
Page* coal ink pads • *ColorBox Cat's Eye* fluid chalk
(Amber Clay, Rouge, Prussian Blue)

1. Stipple and dab inks on page. Stamp letters, wings and cut them out. Stamp doll images close together. **2.** Cut around the doll images and score and fold between the dolls. Stamp game piece letters close together, then cut around them. **3.** Score and fold at the same folds as the dolls. **4.** Tape the set of scrabble letters to the dolls. **5.** Cut out baby photos. Arrange and glue wings, then glue baby photos. **6.** Stamp small dolls on page. Glue small wings, letters and photos on two pieces of cardstock which has a hinged left side. **7.** Create a hinge by scoring and folding 1/2" from the edge. Tape cardstock to the book page. Tape the first doll onto the open flap, then tape the last doll on the book page.

Pop-Ups... Use Paper to Make a Tent

A tent always makes someone smile. It's in the middle of two pages and the fold of the tent has to be lined up with the spine of the book. The object *that pops-up needs to be the general size of a long rectangle set on its side (think hot dog bun). And it is important to be sure your object isn't so long that it sticks out of your book when closed.*

Tent Fold Pattern

Fold   Fold   Fold

1. Stamp a shape onto cardstock. Draw a tab on each side, about 1/2" wide. Cut around the shape and tabs. **2.** Make a Mountain Fold in the center, and fold tabs. Fold the left tab back (behind the shape). **3.** Fold the right tab forward (in front of the shape).

Pop -Ups make altering your pages fun!

Making the Tent for the Tent of Women

1. Glue handmade papers over both pages. **2.** Make the tent itself by gluing the clip art women to cardstock. **3.** Draw tabs on either side of the women. **4.** Cut women and tabs out. **5.** Fold women in half, Mountain Fold, so both halves are even. Score and fold tabs in Mountain Folds. Score. **6.** Position tent over spine of book. Double-check so the tent doesn't stick out when the

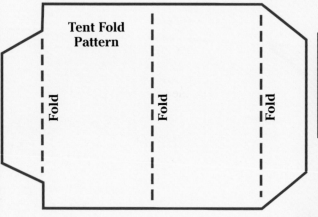

Pop-Ups...
Use Fibers to Make a Tent

Use a sparkly thread called blending filament that is strong. When you open the pages the rays simply pop off the page.

Golden Rays
by Joy Bathie

The golden rays are made with a crinkly thread. Look closely, it is always a pleasant surprise to open these pages.

MATERIALS: Sequin waste ribbon • 1/8" eyelets • Sequins • Paste Paper • *Kreinik* Blending Filament, Gold 002 • Gesso and paints
1. Gesso and paint the pages. Tear paste paper into a rectangle. Tear a piece off the rectangle. **2.** Set eyelets around one edge of the rectangle and the piece that is torn. **3.** Glue the middle of rectangles onto the page and let it dry. Sew the rectangle parts together gently with Blending Filament. **4.** Make rays that attach to the opposite page and glue to page. Glue a strip of sequin waste ribbon to page.

'Time' Hand Book
by Tracie Miser

Tracie Miser shows us that we can also put a tent inside a board book. It's fun!

MATERIALS: Hand book • Cardstock • Computer generated words • *ColorBox Cat's Eye* fluid chalk in Amber Clay • *Golden* Regular Gel Matte
1. Collage papers on pages. **2.** Do 'direct to paper' over collage with Amber Clay Cat's Eye chalks. **3.** Find an image to pop-up and construct a tent by folding the image out. **4.** Make small tabs to glue on the back of image. Glue tabs to back of tent and let dry. **5.** Glue the other side of tab to page.

Tent of Women
by Meg Malvasi

MATERIALS: Clip art women • Computer generated quotes • Handmade papers

book is closed. **7.** Position and glue women on pop-up tent. **8.** Glue one end of tab to book. **9.** Completely fold tent in half. Place glue on the top of second tab and shut book. Tab will be placed in the perfect spot on the second page.

Flying Girl Pop-Up

by Beth Cote

Try this colorful, interactive page in several versions and color combinations. The pop-up girl in the center is always a fun surprise.

MATERIALS: Cardstock • Image • Handmade papers • *Golden* Quinacridone Red Fluid Acrylic • *Lumiere* Gold paint by *Jacquard*

DESIGN GIRL: Cut out a girl. Follow the steps under 'Pop-Ups... Basic Angle Fold.

FINISH PAGE: Glue handmade papers and music over pages. Mask off text that you want to save. Paint pages with Red fluid acrylics. Let dry. Dab gold *Lumiere* paint through screening. Let dry.

Pop-Ups... Basic Angle Fold

I love the angle fold because it is a way to extend the page upward. The key to this structure is to be sure that the pop-up image isn't too tall for your book and be sure the image has a general half circle shape.

It is also important to have some excess cardstock to act as a balance to the part of the pop-up that extends above the page. These pages are always really fun to open.

1. Glue image to cardstock. Eyeball image and mentally draw a half circle. **2.** Cut out. **3.** At the halfway point make a Valley Fold vertically, so the image is inside fold. **4.** Leave the image folded in half and place on page with the fold in spine. Experiment with folding the image from the spine of the book down across to the outside edge at a right angle. All parts of the image should be inside the book. **5.** Fold an Angle Fold both forward and back and score well with a bone folder. **6.** Push the image forward with your finger so the top part of the image goes into the folded base. **7.** Glue two sets of two pages together in your book. These will be the strong pages that you will glue this structure to. Open the glued sets of pages so you have one set on each side of the book, like bread for a sandwich. The top of this structure should be glued about 1" from the top of the page. Do not glue anywhere above the fold. Collage papers over extra cardstock and pages that show.

Extended Windows

Jail Uniform Cover

In Altered Books 101, we made a simple window. For this book cover, stamp a Postmodern Design jail uniform on paper then glue it onto the cover. Cut a window through it and glue a face on the inside page.

Peeking Eye

In 101, we also looked at filled windows. In this example, use Maryruma or mulberry paper to fill a punched window, then tear papers to collage around the window. Finish the project with a small brass frame. Now layer your windows.

Stacked Windows
by Beth Cote

This project pulls great ideas into an extravagant multi-page structure. Try these interactive ideas for a fun sequence of pages.

MATERIALS: *Autumn Leaves* Paper and Vellum • *ColorBox Cat's Eye* inks • *Lumiere* paints • *American Tag* envelope and tags • *Hero Arts* little envelope and card • *JudiKins* stamped image (either Layered Frame #2577J or Layered Jewel Frame #2575J) • Assorted background stamps • *Limited Edition* game piece letters or words

1. Stamp frames and cut out three frames. Be sure to match the circle you cut on both frames. Cut out the middle hole. **2.** Collage the background with papers. **3.** Glue frame to first page and cut a hole in one page. **4.** Center frame on second page and cut a hole in two pages. **5.** Carefully rip around frame and collage the edge with *Cat's Eye* Chestnut Roan fluid chalk. **6.** Stamp and glue a little envelope on page. **7.** Center the third frame in hole and cut through one page. **8.** Collage the last page. Do 'direct to paper' on all three pages with *Cat's Eye* inks. Add *Lumiere* paint for accents. Rip the tag envelope. Glue to page and glue on letter tiles. Place tag in envelope.

Angle Fold Pattern

Fold along dashed lines.

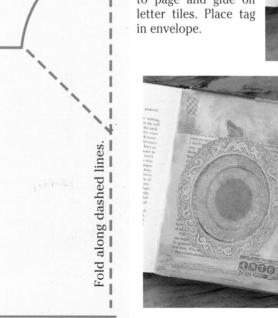

Pull Tabs... Basic Pull Tab

A pull tab is an exciting element for a book. The movement always makes people smile. You need two images... one that is seen and the surprise element that is hidden until the tab is pulled. It is best that they relate to the page in some way. I like to play with imagery and color as well as words.

1. Trace and cut out two pull tab paddles. Glue a Flower image on half of pull tab that is closest to paddle end. The first image that will always show when the tab is not pulled is the one closest to the handle of the paddle. Punch a 1" circle in the bottom half of tab. **2.** Glue two pages together. Collage black and white image over the page. Cut a 1 inch square on the glued page in your book. The square should be centered unless you have a very large book. **3.** Place your paddle on the page behind the window you glued. Check to see if your paddle has enough room to move up and down on the page. Center the image closest to paddle handle in the window and draw a line flush with the bottom of the paddle. **4.** Move the paddle, so the second image shows through the window. Mark the top of the paddle in this position flush. Figure out where hole lines up with the page. Glue a computer generated quote to page so it shows through the hole. **5.** Draw two lines on each side of the paddle with about $1/16$" wiggle room so the paddle can move. These are your glue guidelines. **6.** I like to use *Peel n Stick*™ double-sided adhesive sheet. It is a nice heavy-duty adhesive that reinforces the page. I lay a sheet over my guidelines and draw them on one side of the tape. Cut around the guidelines so the paddle channel is clear. Peel the backing from one side and lay it on the page. **7.** Be sure to place the paddle in its channel. **8.** Peel the tape from the other side of the adhesive. Double-check that paddle is in channel and no tape is near it. Place window page over adhesive and press firmly. Trim paddle length and punch hole in handle. Add fibers to paddle.

Change Images with Peek a Boo Pull Tabs!

A Child's Eye
by Beth Cote

Pull tabs make everyone's pulse quicken. What is hidden beyond our sight? This technique is easy once you do it a couple of times.

MATERIALS: Pull tab pattern • Craft Knife • Cutting Mat • Metal Ruler • Images or stamps for pull tab • *Peel n Stick* double-sided adhesive sheet • *Kreinik* fibers for pull tab

1. Glue two pages together. Cut a 1" square on the glued page in your book. The square should be centered unless you have a very large book. Follow the instructions above.

A Hidden Treasure

by Joyce Yuen

We all have played with a jack-in-the-box and smiled every time Jack popped out. Here is a grown-up version of this idea. You can have anything pop out, but remember there should be a reason or some tie-in to the meaning of the theme. This is a beautiful layout that uses playing cards as the base for the pull tabs.

STAMP CREDITS: *Stampendous* Marble Cube • *Stampers Anonymous* Alphabet • *Art Dreams* Women • *All Night Media/Anna Griffin* ribbon • *Ancient Page* coal ink pads, *ColorBox Metalextra* Peacock Blue ink pad • *ColorBox Cat's Eye* fluid chalk (Amber Clay, Yellow Ochre, Rouge, Burnt Sienna)

Mask text. Stipple inks onto page and stamp Marble Cube. Paint Black Gesso on back of playing cards and let dry. Stamp letters and images and cut out. Stamp ribbon image on $1^5/8$" x 4" cardstock. Score and fold one quarter of the way down from the top of the women images, fold and glue top to the playing card. Tape the bottom of images to the ribbon image. Cut 1" x $2^1/8$" Black cardstock. Score and fold in half to create a hinge. Tape edge of playing a card to hinge and tape the other edge to book page. Make a $1^1/2$" slit on the book page, approximately $2^1/2$" from the top edge of each playing card. The ribbon image will slide into the slit. Cover slit area with 1" of a playing card. Use tape on three sides of the playing card. Glue letters to playing cards and add eyelets.

Pull Tabs... A Jack-in-the-Box

You can make a lot of different pull tabs. Here are two other methods for making a pull tab that is attached to a folded card or playing card. This is a fun method that reminds me of a jack-in-the-box. It is important to make sure that glue or any paint doesn't get on the moving parts.

1. Stamp an image or part of an image on cardstock. I like to keep in mind the image of a Jack-in-the-Box. **2.** Draw lines down from the bottom of the stamped image. The length of the rectangle you add is about the length it will pull up when opened. I usually add the same amount as the height of the stamped image plus $3/4$". You need to add tabs on the end of the rectangle. These will act as a stop when the image is pulled open. I usually add tabs that are about $3/4$" thick and 1" long on both sides. **3.** Fold a piece of cardstock in half. Glue to page. Make a slit in the cardstock and through the book page that is slightly larger than the base of your pop-up, not the tabs, just the area that is going to slide up and down. **4.** Hold pop-up where the stamped image meets the base in a Valley Fold. Fold the tabs over and slip the base of the pop-up into the slit. Turn page over and open tabs. Tabs are kept open. **5.** Glue top of head to the folded piece of cardstock. To figure correct placement, fold image over, put glue on back of head and fold cardstock over image. Press. **6.** Add Peel n Stick double-sided adhesive tape either $1/4$" or $1/8$" around the outside of cardstock or page and back with page in book to hide pop-up tabs.

Suspended Hand

When you suspend something in a window, it tends to move and jingle with the book. It adds romance to a plain cover. You can use anything to suspend the object. I used wire but have used beaded chains, thin beading wires, fibers, metal chains and fishing line.

MATERIALS: *American Tag* hand tag • *Limited Edition* Alphabet stamp • Gold embossing powder • *ColorBox* Gold pigment ink • Black cardstock • *Design Originals Legacy Collage* Dictionary paper • Black 3/16" eyelets • Wire • *Lumiere* Halo Violet paint • *Neopaque* White & Black. paint • *AMACO* Rub 'n Buff (Antique Gold, Copper) **1.** Punch four holes and add eyelets to the hand tag. I punched holes and set the eyelets using the extended eyelet setter and punch from *American Tag*. **2.** Cut a hole in the cover of your book about 1/4" to 1/8" larger than the hand on all sides. **3.** Punch four 3/16" holes in your book that line up with the eyelets on the hand. **4.** Paint book with *Lumiere* paints. Be kind of dry with the paint, better to cover in two coats than to be liberal with the paint. **5.** Rub a bit of *Lumiere* on the hand. Stamp alphabet on cardstock and emboss. Rub a bit of *Rub 'n Buff* on the alphabet that is embossed and glue to hand. **6.** Cut wire into four pieces and thread hand into window. **7.** Collage behind hand with Dictionary paper.

How to Make Your Titles Pop!

One of the most important things about an altered book is its theme. The title is a perfect way to convey the theme without hitting your viewer over the head with a brick. So, it is best to spend some time thinking, viewing and playing with different titles and ways to put them on your cover.

Game pieces are an easy way to spell out your title. You can buy small metal letters in craft stores that have fun shapes as well. I like the faux typewriter keys that Coffee Break Designs has to give a great old world look to your book without that blow torch! (Ever try to get the real metal keys off a typewriter??? It isn't easy!)

Alphabet stamps are an easy way to get a great look and feel to your title. Several unique fonts and sizes are available. Red Line Letters use a see-thru system that lets you line the alphabet up and stamp words and phrases at the same time. Hot Potatoes has several fun large alphabets and Postmodern Design has extended their spindle system to include alphabet stamps (a great way of keeping everything together).

by
Wendy Vecchi

Helpful Hint:
When stamping titles, remember to use *StazOn, Ancient Page, Brilliance* or *Memories* ink over collage elements and acrylic paints.
Be sure to heat set your inks.

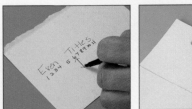

Stamping Titles - 1. Write a word or phrase on a piece of scrap paper. Count the letters and spaces. **2.** Find the mid-point of your phrase. Measure where you want the title to be and figure the midpoint of where you want to stamp your words. **3.** Make a sample the same width of your book on scrap paper. Always stamp the words on scrap paper first to work out any kinks of the title. Start with the middle of your phrase and the middle of your space and work outward. Always work with a ruler below the words to help space the letter and keep the stamps straight. Feel free to move the letter slightly to give it an old world or eclectic look. **4.** Stamp on your book in same manner.

Arrows and Spinners

I love things that spin. Movement energizes your altered book pages and can really add a punch to page layouts. You can use either plastic or metal arrows that come from American Tag or make your own spinner.

PREMADE SPINNER - If you are using an arrow from *American Tag*, be sure to place the arrow with the concave cup facing up onto matboard or your page. Set an eyelet inside of the cup. The concave shape raises the ends of the arrow slightly so it can spin easily.

MAKE YOUR OWN SPINNER - Stamp an image onto cardstock and cut out. Find the center of the image and punch a $1/8$" hole in center. Use a long stem eyelet and washer. Layer the matboard, washer, stamped spinner and eyelet. Loosely set the eyelet through everything to allow it to spin.

Choices
by Beth Cote

This book's title and theme are carried further by including a spinning arrow on the cover. It is one of my favorite covers and is simple to make.

1. Cover a small piece of mat board with text paper. Punch a hole in matboard with an extended eyelet setter and punch a $3/16$" circle. Run a silver pen over edges of matboard. 2. Collage book cover with papers. 3. Run a Black *Memories* ink pad over corners and edges of book. 4. Stamp title with *Hot Potatoes* Cool Man alphabet. 5. Place arrow in hole and glue to book.

MATERIALS: *American Tag* arrow spinner • $3/16$" Eyelet • *Limited Edition* collage clips • *Design Originals* Legacy paper #0497 TeaDye letters • *Memories* Black ink • Matboard • *Pentech* Silver pen • *Hot Potatoes* Cool Man alphabet

Elizabeth's Travels
by Beth Cote

I love using dollhouse doors, windows, moldings and elements in my altered books. Be sure to visit a hobby store that specializes in dollhouses and trains. You will be surprised at all the cool things you will find.

MATERIALS: *Design Originals Legacy Collage* papers (#0552 Elizabeth's Travels, #0418 Love Letters) • *Seven Gypsies* Mille Paper • White Gesso

MATERIALS: Dollhouse window • *Artchix Studio* clip art • Craft knife, cutting mat, pencil, metal ruler • *Uhu* glue stick or *Golden* regular gel matte • *Golden* fluid acrylics • Sandpaper

1. Gesso book cover. Let Dry. 2. Draw a square to fit your dollhouse window on the cover of your book. Using a heavy-duty craft knife with a new blade, lightly run the knife around the rectangle. Use a metal ruler as a guide and do not press hard, rather use light repeated strokes. Cut through the cover of your book. 3. Rip papers. Glue to gessoed book cover. 4. Rub *Golden* fluid acrylics, then buff into the edges. Sand the edges for a more distressed look.

Crackle Cover
by Beth Cote

This romantic book cover seems to have a women peering through chucks of plaster. A rusty keyhole is just off-center. It is simple to do, but needs to dry for two days for the crackle to completely set.

MATERIALS: *US ArtQuest* 101 Crackle Medium • *Golden* fluid acrylic (Transparent Red oxide, Carbon Black) • *Golden* Raw Umber Glaze • Gloss Polymer Medium Image Transfer (see page 47) • Plastic Gloves to protect your hands • Bowl • Plastic knife

1. Paint book Black and let dry. Glue an image transfer element to book cover. **2.** Mix 101 Crackle Medium with Transparent Red Oxide to tint. I used about three squirts of the Red Oxide in about 1/4 cup of crackle medium. **3.** Ice the book and spine with crackle medium with the plastic knife. Wear gloves. **4.** Let dry overnight. Use a light coat of Raw Umber to stain the Crackle Medium further. **5.** Let dry completely for two days.

Stucco Door
by Beth Cote

Lori Wilson shared this great stone look with me. It is created with Golden Fine Artist Colors for a wonderful faux door that can be opened and closed.

MATERIALS: An unloved hardcover book • Pencil • Heavy-duty craft knife • Metal ruler • Cutting mat • Gesso • Black high pigmented acrylic paint • *Houseworks* Carolina dollhouse door, door knob and key plate • *Golden* fluid acrylic paints (Red Oxide, Interference Green Oxide, Carbon Black) • *Golden* Raw Sienna matte fluid acrylic • *Golden* Glaze (Slate, Burnt Sienna, Raw Umber) • *Golden* Garnet Gel Fine • *Golden* Heavy Molding Paste • *Golden* regular gel matte • Soft paint brush or Mop brush • Plastic knife or plastic palette knife • Foam plates • Rag • Clip art • *Coffee Break Design* small rectangular frame • *Krylon* matte spray sealer

1. Draw a rectangle the same size as the doll house door on the cover of your book. Using a heavy-duty craft knife with a new blade, lightly run the knife around the rectangle. Use your metal ruler as a guide and do not press hard, rather use light repeated strokes. Cut through the cover of book and into book if your door is thicker than the cover. **2.** Paint your door with gesso then with *Golden* fluid acrylic in Red Oxide. Sponge on Interference Green Oxide and Raw Sienna for highlights. Dry brush Carbon Black around the edges of the door. Let dry.

Butterfly Wings

by Jackie Hull

MATERIALS: Old lace • Buttons • Key charms • Collage papers • Vintage photo • *Limited Edition* numbers • *All Night Media* mirror saying • *Stamp Art Jubilee* secrets, butterfly wings • *ERA Graphics* fibers • Optical lens • Vellum • Cardstock (Eggplant, Mauve, Khaki, Light Blue) • *ColorBox* Copper ink pad • *Memories* Black ink pad • *JudiKins* Diamond Glaze • *Tombow* markers

1. Color your vintage stamp. 2. Mat photo stamp in three layers using Eggplant, Mauve and Light Blue cardstock. Run Copper ink over Light Blue edges. 3. Add two more layers with Ochre Vellum, let edges hang off end. Glue together with matted photo stamped image and rip edges of Vellum. 4. Collage text over Khaki cardstock and layer. Glue all mats on top of this layer. Stamp numbers. 5. Glue more collage text on Eggplant cardstock and use text stamps to give abstract background. Layer another piece of Vellum. Glue together and let dry. 6. Glue Eggplant cardstock to book cover. Glue buttons, lace, and knotted fibers to book cover. 7. Stamp 'secrets' and 'butterfly wings' on scraps of cardstock and vellum. Glue to book. Using Diamond Glaze, glue optical lens to cover. Add key charm and threads.

Women with Wolves

by Beth Cote

Women love adventure... here that theme is dear to the hearts of creative women who participated in a Round Robin.

3. Paint Gesso on the book covers and spine. Paint book with Black acrylic paint. Let dry. 4. Mix $1/4$ cup *Golden* Garnet Gel Fine with $1/4$ cup *Golden* Heavy Molding Paste. Apply mix to cover of book with a plastic knife or palette knife. It is like frosting a cake, but you want the texture uneven for a stone appearance. Place the door in the hole and let dry overnight. 5. Squirt out *Golden* Glaze in Burnt Sienna and Raw Umber on a plate. Use a paint brush to pick up both colors and dab over surface. Wipe off with a rag as you work to blend colors. Continue until you like the colors you have on your texture. Apply a bit of Slate to plate. Dab a small amount of Slate over texture and use it to highlight and deepen fissures. 6. Glue on collage material behind door. Add embellishments. 7. Seal cover with *Krylon* spray sealer in matte.

MATERIALS: Vintage photo of woman • Decorative Papers • *Postmodern Design* alphabet stamp set • *Brilliance* Gold ink pad • *Books by Hand* PVA

1. Cut papers 2" larger than book cover. Glue to book cover with PVA. I butted the decorative paper up to the cloth spine of the book itself and then glued. 2. Cut out face and glue to page as well. Stamp title down the cloth spine and heat set ink.

3. This was a Round Robin and had a tag sign-in. All the tags hanging down from the spine were signed by the artists who participated in this Round Robin.

'Life 1O1' Book Cover
by Beth Cote

Masking tape makes a great textured background. You can change that texture by either ripping sections of tape off the roll and piecing them together or using long strips like this book cover. I also added 'Tape Transfers' to the cover. 'Tape Transfers' are also called 'Cold Laminate Transfers' (find out about them on page 43).

MATERIALS: Masking tape • Tape transfers • *Golden* fluid acrylics (Transparent Red Oxide, Quinacridone Burnt Orange, Quinacridone Crimson) • *Neopaque* Black paint by *Jacquard* • Dry wall tape (has small dots in it and you can find it in a home supply store) • *Krylon* clear spray sealer

1. Paint the book with Black paint and let dry. **2.** Rip long strips of tape off the roll and apply them to the cover of the book randomly. **3.** Glue 'Tape Transfers' on over masking tape and cover edges with more masking tape. **4.** Continue to add tape. Don't forget the spine and back of the book. **5.** With a brush apply Transparent Red Oxide fluid acrylic over both the tape and 'Tape Transfers'. With a damp cloth, wipe off excess. Continue this across the book cover. **6.** Repeat with Quinacridone Burnt Orange and Crimson. **7.** Dry brush book with Black paint. Rub through the paint so some tape shows. Wipe excess paint off 'Tape Transfers'. Let dry. **8.** Seal with Krylon Spray Sealer. This will not only protect your cover but marry the different sheens the tapes give off. Don't forget this step, it makes a difference.

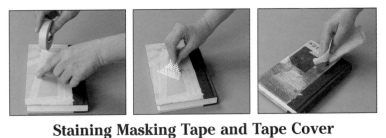

Staining Masking Tape and Tape Cover

1. Layer masking tape over book cover. **2.** Lay 'Tape Transfers' over masking tape. Add bits of drywall tape. **3.** Paint fluid acrylics over tape, wipe off with a damp rag.

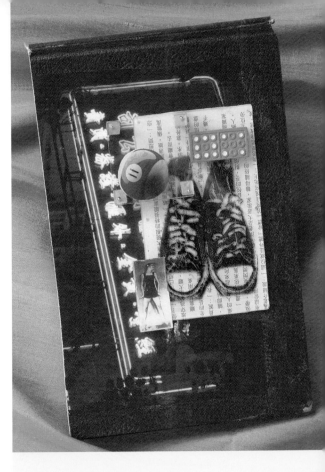

'Yin' Book Cover
by Beth Cote

Yin is one half of a duo altered book that is called Yin and Yang. I turned a large book on its edge and cut it in half to make the duo. The on-the-edge feel of the night is amplified by the acrylic piece used to give dimension to this book cover. This is one of my favorite pieces and I love the 3-D effect.

MATERIALS: *Coffee Break Design* 2" x 2" and 3" x 5" acrylic pieces • Plastic microscope plates • *Postmodern Design* Old Sneakers Stamp • Alphabet cube beads • 4 Brass trim nails • Collage materials • *Lumiere* Black paint • An old Atlas to cut in half • *Limited Edition* Green domino from Altered Book Kit • *JudiKins* Diamond Glaze • *Memories* ink pad

Preparing the book: **1.** Paint cover Black and collage an image across the front. Cut book in half with a scroll saw. **2.** Turn the book on its side, so it opens from the bottom. **3.** Prepare the large acrylic piece separately. Stamp with *Memories* ink on the acrylic piece and carefully heat set the ink; the piece might buckle so be prepared to bend it back. **4.** Glue the pool ball image to the back of the small acrylic piece with Diamond Glaze. Glue oriental text to the back of the large acrylic piece. **5.** Take a small slide and glue it on the woman image. After it dries, cut the image and slide out of paper and trim the slide. **6.** Make the legs for the small acrylic piece: Take the four brass trim nails and dip one end of each in Diamond Glaze. Coat the top of all the cube beads and place each bead under the nail holes. Stick each nail in each hole in small acrylic piece and cube beads and let dry. **7.** Coat the bottom of the beads with Diamond Glaze and glue to the book cover. Glue the domino to the cover with Diamond Glaze and let dry.

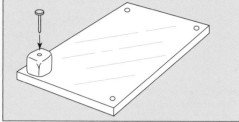

Acrylic Sheet

Use a pin or a tiny nail in a wood cube or wood bead to secure the small acrylic sheet to the book cover.
1. Coat a pin and wood cube bead with Diamond Glaze. **2.** Slip pin in each hole on top of acrylic piece and into hole in each cube.

Sea Song

by Beth Cote

The calm of the sea is apparent here in this quiet book cover. A mermaid floats over a collaged sea with a compass to guide her way. The circles in the collage are used again in the title and in the beads, compass and screws to create a rhythm with little round elements.

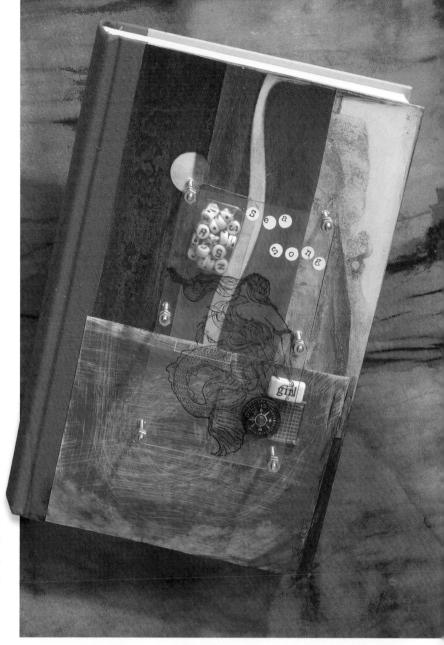

1. Drill holes in the book cover with a hand drill or cordless drill. **2.** Thread each screw from the back of book to the front. **3.** Set all six nuts at the same height from book cover on the six screws. **4.** Set acrylic piece on top of nuts. **5.** Screw the second set of nuts on top of the acrylic piece.

MATERIALS: *Beadery* Alphabet beads • Computer generated title • 1/8" hole punch • 6 screws and 12 nuts • *Coffee Break Designs* 4" x 6" acrylic piece • Compass • Sand Paper • *Stampers Anonymous* Word Tile • See through plastic packaging form • *Golden* Regular Gel Matte • *Time to Stamp* Mermaid stamp • *Memories* Black ink pad • *Peel n Stick* double-sided adhesive
1. Collage Blue papers to cover the cover. Let dry. Gently rub sandpaper in a circle on the bottom of cover to create texture.
2. Mark holes from acrylic piece to cover and drill. **3.** Stamp mermaid on acrylic piece with *Memories* Black ink. Heat set. **4.** Type the title of altered book on computer and print. Use a circle punch to punch out letters and glue onto acrylic piece. **5.** Place alphabet beads on plastic form. Place *Peel n Stick* double-sided adhesive all around the lip of the plastic cup-like form. Decide placement of the form. Carefully flip the cup-like form onto the book and press around edges to seal the tape. **6.** Thread all six screws through back of book. Follow the instructions above to attach the acrylic piece. **7.** Use *Peel n Stick* double-sided adhesive to adhere the compass and word tile to cover under the acrylic piece.

Flaps, Folds, Overlays and Envelope Closures

Part of the unique part of altered books is that you are using a pre-bound book in place of a series of collages to be hung on the wall. As altered book artists, it is our duty to manipulate this structure to our advantage. One way of doing this is to segment parts or pages of the book off to make them special. You can do this in a themed way, like special chapters. You can do this to mark a certain structures or in a Round Robin (see page 48) to display one artist's work like a mini portfolio.

Another way to add punch to a page is by either adding space to the page with a flap or overlay. These are manipulative structures which means that people move them to reveal something. If you are working in a book with little space, this is a great way to give yourself more work room. But beyond that reason, by drawing attention to the structure, you set the art in this piece apart denoting it as something different or special, and people will take a bit more notice of what is there, underneath or on the next page. Be sure to place your flaps on all sides of the page, not just what is normal. The unexpected is the best way to make your pages pop.

OPEN FLAP   OPEN THE FLAP   FLAP   OPEN THE FLAP   OPEN FLAP

'Prologue' Folding Flap

by Beth Cote

This little flap comes over a section of the book and contains several pages. Use this structure sparingly, because its strength will be diminished with repeated use in the same book.

All the pages contained in the flap need to have some kind of bond, be it a poem, color, theme or artist.

MATERIALS: *AMACO* Copper metal mesh 50080H • *American Tag* merchandise tag • Cardstock • *ColorBox Cat's Eye* fluid chalk and ink pads • *Limited Edition* Tag alphabet • *Hero Arts* Printer Type alphabet • Rivets • *American Tag* eyelet and rivet setter and punch

1. To prepare metal, I held the metal wire mesh over a hot flame to color it. 2. Fold edges back with a ruler. 3. Stamp words on tag and glue to metal. 4. Score and fold 4" from one end of the paper. Score and fold another line 4$^{1}/8$" from one end of the paper. 5. Glue the 4" between two pages. Match the first fold with the outside edge of the page. 6. Fold the paper over pages until comfortable. 7. Glue mesh in place. Punch with $^{1}/8$" circle punch. 8. Rivet the corners. 9. 'Direct to paper' fluid chalk and ink on cardstock and page. Stamp alphabet randomly across the page.

'Guitar' Folding Flap Page by Randy Keenan

Randy uses her computer to generate beautiful background collages then she manipulates further with text, drawings, sewing and overlays. Guitar has a flap that has been cut to emphasize the shape of the guitar.

MATERIALS: Computer generated collage or collage papers • Cardstock • Colored gel pens • White gel pen • Black gel pen • Mulberry paper • *Uhu* Glue stick • Bone folder

1. Use a computer to generate the background and guitar. Print two copies. Glue one to your page. If you do not use a computer, collage a background on your page and either draw or create the guitar shape. Make a color copy of this collage. **2.** Back the color copy or second computer print with cardstock. This will be the front of your flap. Decide which side will be the hinge and cut out the curve of the guitar on the opposite side. **3.** Cut your mulberry paper 1" wide by the exact length of your flap. This will be your hinge. Fold and score with a bone folder. **4.** Glue one side of the mulberry paper to the flap and the other side to the edge of your book page. Make sure they line up neatly and can open and close easily. **5.** Take pieces of cardstock and gel pens and accent the collage with writing, doodling and shapes. You can string real thread for the guitar strings to further embellish your collage.

Making Hinges

1. Cut cardstock to the size and shape of your flap. Cut a 1" wide hinge to fit the flap. Fold mulberry paper in half and score with a bone folder.

2. Glue one side of hinge, place hinge of cardstock at the edge.
3. Apply glue to other side of hinge. Place in book and press firmly.

Hidden Hinges... Secure Flap Between Two Pages

1. Decide what your flap shape will be and what side will be the hinge. Add 1¹/8" to your hinged side. Cut out. **2.** Fold and score at 1¹/8" and at 1". **3.** Glue the flap onto page, make sure the fold is slightly hanging over the edge of page. **4.** Glue page in front of flap onto the flap page to hide the hinge and strengthen the page. Flap should now flip over the glued page

Tip: Don't feel that your flaps have to have straight edges. Part of the beauty of this piece is the curved edge of the flap.

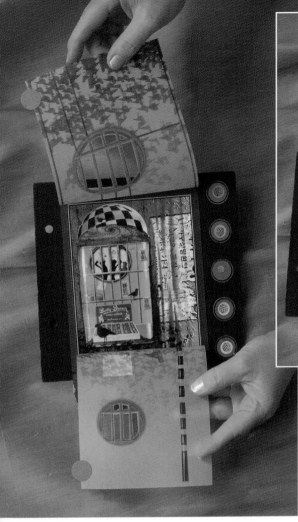

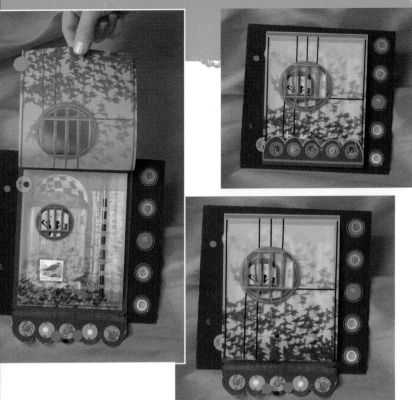

Clever Cages... Folded Pages

This gorgeous layout actually has three different structures in it; an envelope closure and two overlays. The envelope flap is secured with a bit of velcro, since it flips up over the overlays.

Clever Cages Book

by Randy Keenan

MATERIALS: Circle punches in graduated sizes • Two computer generated overlays printed on vellum • Collage materials • Printed vellum • Black cardstock • Window stamp • *StazOn* ink pad • One hinged scalloped envelope closure • 1/16" glossy Black tape • Craft knife • Cutting mat • Metal ruler • *Uhu* glue stick • Tape for vellum

1. Collage with various materials on a separate piece of paper. **2.** You need two vellum overlays for this structure. One overlay opens from the top, one from the bottom. Both overlays will be the same size as your collage, slightly smaller than your page. They are glued with a piece of vellum tape at the edge of the page and unlike a flap, overlays have no true hinge, instead they bend out. **3.** Design two overlays on vellum and cut holes out of the vellum using a craft knife (or use printed vellums). Stamp your window stamp onto the vellum with *StazOn* ink and cut out with a craft knife once it dries overnight. Make a second overlay with another piece of vellum and cut another window freehand that complements your first window. The second overlay will be underneath the first and needs to be 1/4" shorter than the first, so you can adhere the first one to the collage. Put your overlays aside for now. **4.** Make an envelope closure. Trace the envelope closure on cardstock. The closure needs to be as long as the overlay and the collage, so extend it if you need to. Cut out. This has a hidden hinge so go ahead and score and fold 1" on the length of the closure. Punch holes in the scallops and decorate with punched rings of colored cardstock and images printed on vellum. Cut strips of cardstock to decorate further. **5.** Make more circle medallions to decorate the edges of design. **6.** Assemble the completed structure, by backing your page with Black cardstock. Glue. **7.** Double-check collage and vellum overlays. They should all be the same width and fit on the page. If they don't, trim them. The vellum overlay nearest to the collage needs to be 1/4" shorter than the other. **8.** Glue the hidden hinge from the envelope closure to the back of the collage piece. Neither will show when glued to the page. Make sure that the closure is on the bottom of the collage piece so it opens in the right direction. Glue the collage piece with the hinge behind it on the Black cardstock. When gluing, fold the envelope closure up so the front doesn't get glue on it. **9.** Use vellum tape to adhere vellum overlays to collage. Lay the last one down first. It needs to be slightly shorter so the second one can be taped to the collage as well. Lay the first one over it and adhere. **10.** Decorate with glossy tape, medallions, and cardstock strips. **11.** The envelope closure should flip over the overlays. Use a bit of Velcro to keep it attached and add little circles with directions if you don't feel people will understand to lift your layers.

Tip: I love *Sheer Heaven*. It is a vellum that can be printed in your ink jet and will not run. You can stamp on it, color wash over it without it wrinkling, use walnut inks, etc. It is very strong and will not rip. *Sheer Heaven* makes overlays that last forever.

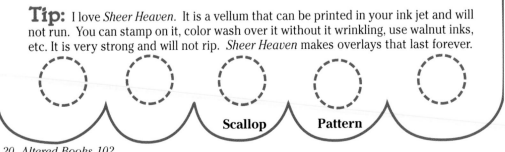

Scallop   Pattern

Dream
by Joy Bathie

In these light and airy pages, an envelope closure opens up to reveal a flap underneath. It is quite a strong and large structure giving the appearance of a book inside a book.

Materials: Gesso • Tissue papers • Collage material • Cardstock

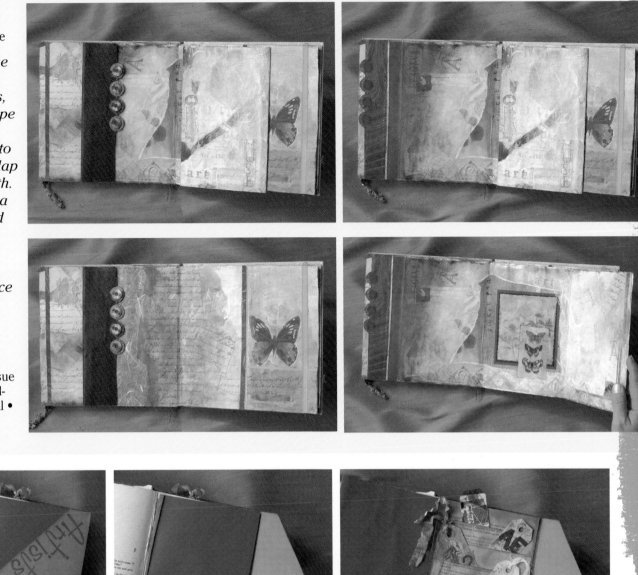

Artist Credit Envelope
by Beth Cote

Create a series of fun-to-open flaps in great colors.

MATERIALS: Old book at least 7" high • Three pieces of cardstock • Bone folder or ruler • Border punch • *Hot Potatoes* Cool Man alphabet • Tags • *ColorBox Cat's Eye* fluid chalks (Amber Clay, Chestnut Roan)

1. Cut paper to the width of your book. **2.** Score and fold 4" from one end of the paper. Score and fold another line $4^1/8$" from one end of the paper. **3.** Glue the 4" between two pages. Match the first fold with the outside edge of the page. **4.** Fold the paper over 7 pages. **5.** Cut out an envelope shape to cover the page. Glue the second piece of cardstock to the inside page for strength. Cut a slit for the tab. **6.** Stamp the title with *Hot Potatoes* Cool Man alphabet. **7.** Start at the back to make the pockets inside the envelope. The seventh page is the full length page that the envelope fold is glued between. **8.** You are going to cut every page before the seventh page in increments of 1". Divide it into 7 parts. **9.** Cut the 6th page 1" from the top. Cut the 5th page 2" from the top. Cut the 4th page 3" from the top. Cut the 3rd page 4" from the top. Cut the 2nd page 5" from the top. Cut the 1st page 6" from the top. **10.** Glue pages together from page one going forward. You need to glue the bottom of the page and side to create a pocket. The bottom of the pages need to be glued as deep as the pocket before it. **11.** Add color with 'direct to paper' *Cat's Eye* fluid chalk and stamp. **12.** Put tags in pockets.

Easy Folded Flap

Time as a Bridge

by Beth Cote

Another easy flap uses the back of the preceding page to form an envelope. The whites in this composition add a subtle emotion and the interference violet gives it punch.

Interference colors are fun to work with and quite easy to use. I like to add them after I have completed a page for detail and edging.

Tip: Before I add any color to a piece, I do test it on a scrap piece of paper or leftover collage material to make sure it creates the effect I am looking for.

MATERIALS: Collage materials • *Emagination* Grey textured papers • Silk paper • Quote and chapter words • Gesso • *Golden* fluid acrylics (Bone Black, Interference Violet)
1. Fold left page in half toward the spine. Glue left page from fold to spine to back page to create a flap. 2. Open flap and glue paper to inside of flap to reinforce the flap. 3. Rip and cut papers and images and glue to pages on double spread and inside flap. 4. Pull apart silk paper and glue to collage for texture. 5. Sponge gesso over collage with a wiping motion. Carefully add a bit of Bone Black to plate and sponge a bit on corners. Be sure to work flap and double spread together so they match. 6. Use a screen and lightly sponge through screen with a dry sponge with a bit of Black, on both double spread and inside flap. 7. Sponge Violet on parts of the collage to highlight areas. Add cut text and final collage elements so they stand out.

Circus Art

by Wendy Vecchi

The colors on the banner contrast well with the neutral background, making the banner the focal point of this double spread.

MATERIALS: 5 colors of cardstock • *Ancient Page* ink pads (Sand, Black, Stone, Grey) • Stipple brushes • Assorted stamps
1. Make a banner by cutting triangles out of all five colors of cardstock and gluing them together. Glue the banner either flat to the page or made into a flap with a Mulberry paper hinge. 2. Stipple color on the page starting with the lightest color first. Work into the dark colors. 3. Stamp over the stippled colors. 4. Add bits of punched cardstock for decoration.

'JFK' Book Pages

by Randy Keenan

I love this political piece. It has wonderful visual punch and the flip flop of the transparent overlay adds a huge impact and a double collage. Remember, all art doesn't need to be beautiful. Sometimes the grittier it is, the bigger the impact.

MATERIALS: Transparency Sheet image • *Krylon* Clear Sealer • Collage materials (two that relate to each other somehow) • *JudiKins* Diamond Glaze • *Uhu* glue stick • Cardstock

1. This piece uses two related collages with a "bridge" of a transparency sheet between the two which relates to both collages (this needs to be taken into consideration). The design on the transparency sheet doesn't have to be an image. Words or a poem can be equally effective. Design your transparency image and either have it copied at a copy store or print it on transparency sheet material that is formulated for your printer. Spray your transparency with *Krylon* Sealer and let dry. **2.** Design two collages using the transparency for a visual as you work. Collage two different pieces. The bottom collage needs to be glued into your book flat. **3.** Trim about 1/4" off the top of the second collage. This is the top collage and will be seen first. **4.** Glue the top collage which will be seen first to the page. Since this is an overlay, apply the glue in a thin stripe across the bottom of the collage. There is no hinge here. **5.** Glue or use eyelets to attach the transparency to the book page, using the same technique. This time though, the transparency will be added over both collages and will be attached in a small strip across the top of the page onto the bottom collage and book page.

Printing on Freezer Paper

1. Trim freezer paper to 8 1/2" x 11". **2.** Iron tissue, fabric, napkins and other flimsy papers to the shiny side of freezer paper. Trim carefully. **3.** Find a piece of collage material, clip art, photo or words and create a layout in Word, Word Perfect, a Graphic or Greeting card program. Print on paper. Be sure to orient the paper when going through the printer so the ink is printed on your tissue. **4.** Peel tissue paper off freezer paper and use it in art.

Tip: I often print a lot of images at once (store fabric and tissue on freezer paper).

Computers
and Transparent Papers

It is great fun to create your own overlays and collage materials using your printer. You can easily create overlays with Transparent Sheets, just by scanning old pictures into your computer or using clip art. Another great source of material are collections of clip art from greeting card programs. These programs are also helpful in designing with clip art and adding words. I happen to use Photoshop and Word, but sophisticated overlays can be made with very simple programs.

You can also print on certain brands of vellum paper and give your overlay a misty look. 'Sheer Heaven' is a brand of vellum that will take a crease and can be used for flaps. It is very strong. Glama vellum is another brand that can go into an ink jet printer.

You can also print on pattern pieces, silk organza, muslin, napkins, tissue and other flimsy papers and fabrics by ironing them to freezer paper and then running them through your printer. These transparent collage pieces add great visual effects to your work and are simple to do. I usually will take a couple hours to cut trim and iron a bunch of fabrics and tissues to freezer paper and use them over a period of time.

Courtyard
by Beth Cote

The old world romance of this piece is elevated by the use of a rice paper napkin and pattern pieces. I love to use Petite Facets, which look like a string of beads, but can be cut and glued or attached to a page easily without having to worry about the beads coming off the string.

MATERIALS: Collage material • Rice paper napkin • Pattern piece • Suede leather • *Acey Deucy* Stamp • *StazOn* ink pad • *Kreinik* Blue Petite facets • *Uhu* glue stick
1. Tear pattern pieces and glue over two pages. Glue collage elements on top of pattern pieces. 2. Stamp with *StazOn* ink on suede. Heat set and cut out carefully. 3. Carefully separate napkin, so only one layer remains. Rip into pieces. Glue to collage. 4. Glue more pattern pieces to collage and glue on leather. 5. Glue Blue Facets strand to edge of paper and use pattern pieces to glue over Facets so bits shine out.

Tips for Transparent Sheets

- Remember that when you use a transparent paper, part of what is underneath will show through.
- Napkins come in 2 or 3 ply. Pull them apart and use only the top layer. Double-check yourself. It is easy to miss a layer and have to glue again.
- Pattern pieces are fun to use as a decorative element. You can also stamp detailed stamps on tissue and then use them in your collage if the edges of the collage are uneven and don't permit a good stamping surface.
- Artist tissue is stronger than a normal gift tissue.
- Be careful of colored tissues, some will run if glues or other media touch them. Running is a fun technique when you know it will happen.
- You can make any paper or image transparent by rubbing a bit of boiled linseed oil over the paper and letting it dry.
- Tracing paper is another fun transparent paper and is easy to use. Draw an image and glue it over your collage for fun.

The Hug by Beth Cote

This double-page spread with windows makes use of a graph in the book as a design element. Be sure to find books with interesting graphs and charts... mathematic books, engineering books, and science books are all fun to collage.

MATERIALS: *ColorBox Cat's Eye* ink pads (Olive, Amber, Yellow) • Pattern paper • *Postmodern Design* Cupid, Psyche and Window stamps • *Golden* glazes (Violet Earth and Gold) • Cardstock in a Mustard color • *Memories* Black ink pad
1. Do 'direct to paper' with Cat's Eye inks on a double spread. Stamp window on Mustard cardstock with *Memories* ink and heat set. Rip out window. Glue to one page of double spread. 2. Cut the window out. Be sure to put your cutting mat under the page so you don't cut straight through the page. 3. Put scrap paper under pattern piece. Stamp Psyche onto pattern piece. The ink will bleed a bit underneath pattern paper because it is so thin. 4. Turn page behind window and apply glue to page. Center the stamped image in window and lay over glue. Press down. Don't worry if some wrinkles appear, it is part of the look. 5. Let dry. Apply glaze to pattern paper lightly.

Gluing Transparent Papers - 1. Peel backing off of a napkin to make it single ply. 2. Apply glue to the surface of collage where you want the napkin to be. 3. Apply napkin over glue, rip edges for effect.

Tip: To make napkins more stable, iron to freezer paper (page 23). Do this with magazine images as well to stop them from warping when collaging.

Swimmer
by Helga Strauss

This layout uses a shaker card technique to make a unique background for the swimmer. Sand is layered in a small plastic bag and moves with the book.

MATERIALS: Watercolor Paper • Watercolors and paint brush • Black pen • Hole punch • Ribbon • *Artchix Studio* Swimmer image • *Ziploc* small bag • *Lumiere* Gold paint • *Krylon* Gold marker • Craft knife • Cutting mat

1. Fold watercolor paper in half and cut a circle window through both thicknesses. **2.** With watercolor give a wash over watercolor paper for a background look. With Black pen write around window. Punch four corner holes. **3.** Fill a small 3" x 4" *Ziploc* bag with sand. Do not overfill or fill to top, leave a space so sand can shift. Tape the bag in the middle of folded watercolor paper. Use double-sided tape to close watercolor paper around the bag, not super tight. It needs some loose edges. **4.** Rip edges around page. Edge with *Krylon* marker. Glue card in middle of page and use ribbons to thread through holes for a decorative look. **5.** Cut out and glue swimmer to front of window.

Thinking of You
by Helga Strauss

This layout uses a surprise bit of collage material and a paint chip! Little buttons hold the women in place.

MATERIALS: Paint chip • *Artchix Studio* Collage papers • Buttons • Watercolor paper and brush • Watercolors • *Krylon* Gold Marker • Black fine tip pen • *Uhu* glue stick • *E6000* adhesive

1. Paint an abstract design on watercolor paper and let dry. Rip out. **2.** Glue woman image to paper and write around the image, shadowing the shape of woman. **3.** Cut out rectangle pictures of women. Use *Krylon* Gold marker to edge the rectangle pictures of women. Glue them down with a ripped paint chip over the lower half of cards. **4.** Add buttons. Glue with E6000 adhesive. **5.** Edge page with *Krylon* Gold marker.

Finding Collage Materials

I think the most common question after what kind of glue I prefer is, "Where do you find all your collage materials? I never seem to have enough".

When you begin collaging, you seem to use up your collage supplies super fast. Some people even go into a kind of hoard mode where they are afraid to use their "good" collage elements in fear of never finding another good element again.

Relax! There are endless supplies of collage materials out in the world and you shouldn't feel that you may never find another perfect one again.

There are several options to solve this dilemma. But the worst one is to use this as an excuse not to work or use elements you are drawn to for a certain project.

1. If the elements are 'one of a kind' and valuable to you, color copy them.
2. Pick up paper leaflets, postcards, business cards and brochures. You can use these easily and it is very easy to transform them into new backgrounds.
3. Use magazine pages.
4. Don't throw away junk mail. Envelopes can be used for a spot of color and those endless catalogs can be used for scrap paper if nothing else.
5. Clip art books have great images. I have a just published a collection in *Design Originals* 'The Ephemera Book' that includes images from my private collection in full size.
6. Collage papers are usually themed and companies sell them with many photos on one sheet. They are usually vintage images that have been colored and cleaned up for a great look.
7. Garage sales, estate sales, and thrift stores are always my favorite places to look for collage materials. One person's trash is another's treasure.
8. Don't forget to let friends and neighbors know what you are doing. I have found boxes of old buttons, photos, doodads and match sticks on my front porch, dropped off by people who are cleaning out their attics or basements and thought of me.

Altering Your Collage Materials

Feel in a rut? Sick of your collage material? You can spiff it up and give it a new look by changing it or altering it. Spend an afternoon or evening giving your stuff a face-lift. Glazing or painting images is one way and here are three more. You'll love tinting, staining and crumpling collage materials. Use our imaginations to change or age your collection.

Make them look old and vintage to add character to your creations.

Photo One: Shelley Benjamin likes to roll *Brilliance* inks over old postcards to give them a new look and life. The various shades of color seep through and make them look entirely different. Rip them up and go!

Photo Two: Stamp with *Memories* or *StazOn* inks on magazine pages. Forget the focal points and look at the backgrounds of the photos. Stamping on various backgrounds looks very rich and changes the stamped image.

Photo Three: Spray *Krylon* Webbing Spray over colored paper and cardstock. I like to use both black and gold. Let dry, rip and use. A great faux European paper look for the price of a piece of cardstock.

Photo Four: Take a piece of tissue and find a textured item or stamp. Lay the tissue over the item. Rub glitter crayons or construction crayons over tissue and the image will appear. Dust *Pearl Ex* over image and it will stick to

the crayon for a gold foil look. If you use *Spectra* tissue, lightly sprinkle with water and the colored tissue will run a bit, making the image look old and worn.

Flower Arrangement

by Jill Steffey

Jill dyed the handmade block printed paper at the bottom of the page to match her collage. This is a great way to make a large piece of handmade paper become very versatile.

MATERIALS:
Handmade metallic paper • *ColorBox Ancient Page* dye ink pads • Collage materials • Printed tissue papers • *Loew-Cornell* Spongit #508

1. Dye metallic paper with *Ancient Page* inks. Color by pressing direct from the ink pad with a Loew-Cornell Spongit brush to sponge color to paper. You want to create a varied surface. **2.** Glue printed tissue to page. Cut the woman out and glue to page with additional images and quote. **3.** Rip dyed tissue and glue to the bottom of page to add more texture.

Dye paper: 1. Choose a handmade or specialty paper with a metallic print. The metallic print acts as a resist.

2. Using a *Loew-Cornell* Spongit #508 and *Ancient Page* ink, apply ink to paper. Be sure to use wax paper underneath to protect your surface.
3. Glue to the collage.

Making Your Own Backgrounds

Stuck for inspiration? Sometimes the hardest thing is a blank page. Well, here are several days' worth of ideas to get you off to a great start.

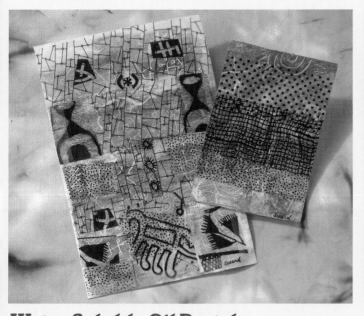

Water Soluble Oil Pastels   by Lynne Sward

Looking for a great bright background?

Take water soluble oil pastels and draw heavy onto your page. Scratch into the pastels with the end of a paint brush so you can see the underneath parts. Work more pastels over the top and continue to scratch through. Print an abstract Black pattern on a Transparency Sheet and glue using *JudiKins* Diamond Glaze to glue over the pastels.

Sanding and Gesso   by Beth Cote

You can turn a collage into instant vintage with a bit of gesso and sandpaper. Collage a map onto a book cover. Sand the cover a bit and layer some *Lumiere* paints by *Jacquard* over the gesso. Sand some more.

With a dry brush, apply a light coat of White gesso. Wipe off. Sand through the layers again as needed for a great effect.

Crumpled Tissue   by Joy Bathie

Crumple a piece of tissue paper. Paint over and under the tissue with Black gesso. The gesso acts like a glue, so move it around as you paint to get the texture you want.

When the tissue paper is dry, tear off excess tissue and go back and paint/glue with Black gesso again. Make lots of wrinkles. Let dry.

Rub with Gold *Rub 'n Buff* by *AMACO*.

Glazed Mono-printing   by Tracie Miser

This technique uses stamps to remove the glaze from a page. This is a reverse mono-print. Wipe your stamp after every imprint. Paint a smooth surface of Plaid's Glaze Varnish in Purple over your page. Stamp with a text stamp into the glaze to lift off the paint. Wipe the stamp with a damp cloth and repeat.

Let dry and wipe a light layer of transparent *Golden* Red Oxide fluid acrylic over the Purple glaze for a deep rich finish.

Starry Night   by Jill Steffey

This background gives a great starry night to lay images against. Play with size here and think fantasy.

1. Paint background with Navy paint and let dry. Glue couple and images to background and flick with a toothbrush dipped in White acrylic paint. Let dry.

Glue on more found collage images and dry brush White paint around the moon to enhance the image. Let dry.

Fluid Acrylics Over Collage   by Beth Cote

This is an easy way to make any background meld together or tint it to any color you choose.

1. Collage a background. Pour *Golden* fluid acrylic color and a bit of matte medium over the surface. Let it set a bit and take your sandpaper and sand through the color.

It has a different look than the gesso and sandpaper, yet still has a bit of a worn look.

Pinata Inks on Hand Book   by Tracie Miser

From the translucent color to the rings of gold, this background is elegant and easy. Be sure to plan a bit as you work on the collage to take advantage of translucent rings.

The brilliant color of these inks makes everything special.

1. Gesso your board book and let dry. Collage images on book. Let dry. Drip Magenta *Pinata Inks* on a sponge. Dab *Krylon* gold marker on the other side of the sponge and dab on book. Move the sponge and continue to dab over and over again. Work fast. When finished drip the *Pinata Extender* straight out of the bottle onto the woman's face. This moves the inks and creates the circle you see. Repeat until the ink is moved to where you like it. Repeat over any other image to highlight it or to highlight words.

Art Doll Page

by Sally Turlington

MATERIALS: *Golden* fluid acrylics (Quinacridone Crimson, Quinacridone Gold, Turquois Phthalo) • White paper • Multi-Use adhesive spreader/scraper or old credit card • Tacky glue or glue stick • *Bond 527* Multi-Purpose Cement or *E6000* • Thin cardboard • Decorative paper • Face, hand, ruler • Collage images • Strips of fabric and fibers • Eyelets • Copper wire • Clock hands, beads, and other 3D embellishments
TO MAKE THE DOLL: Use scraps of paper from other projects to collage a small piece of cardboard for the body. Glue hand images and ruler images to cardboard and cut them out. Use wire to assemble beads, rolled decorative paper beads, and hand images for arms. Use wire to assemble beads, rulers, and clock hands to make legs. Glue the face image to a piece of cardboard and cut out leaving room around the top and sides to punch holes. Pull fabric and fibers through the holes and tie to make the hair. Glue or attach the face, body, hands, and legs to the page allowing the hair, arms and clock hands to hang freely. Embellish the pages with handmade collage pieces and 3D items.

Cemented Background

by Tracie Miser

This earthy background is very versatile. Its texture and rough edges remind me of an archaeological dig. Tint it any color you wish and feel free to embed anything at all in the cement.

This is a great textured background that has bits of collage items floating in it. Mix Golden 101 Cement Heavy with Ochre fluid acrylics in a bowl. Use a knife or plastic spoon and smear the mixture on the page. Float collage items and 3D items in cement. Use the knife to press them into the paste, layer a bit of paste over them.

Bright Colors on Pages

1. Puddle dime-size dots of *Golden* fluid acrylics down one side of a book page, cardstock or glossy paper.

2. Using a piece of matboard draw the acrylic paints across the page, over the spine and over the other page.

3. Continue in the same manner to spread paint on the rest of the page and facing page.

4. Using the excess paint on the matboard, fill in white spots

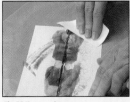

5. When dry, tear or cut colored areas of sheets, punch shapes to use as handmade collage elements.

TIP: For another look, draw *Golden* glaze in a metallic color over a dried colored page and run a comb through it.

Walnut Ink

Tracie Miser loves to use Walnut Inks for texture, images, antiques and more! She is very creative and has unlimited ideas and techniques for using this special liquid ink.

WALNUT INK SPONGED OVER ACRYLIC PAINT

WALNUT INK PAINTED OVER CLEAR RESIST

WALNUT INK WASH

Ancient Artifact
by Mark Frnka

This book feels like someone just dug it out of the ground, the aged appearance due to the use of Walnut Ink.

Add an accent in a niche. Stamp White Paperclay with an image. Allow clay to dry overnight.

MATERIALS: *Postmodern Design* Walnut Ink crystals • *Lumiere* Gold paint • *Ancient Page* ink pads (Black, Sienna) • *Fred B. Mullett* Bamboo Stamp • *Raindrops on Roses* Fern Stamp • *US ArtQuest* Large Leaf • *Toybox* Ancient Artifact stamp • *Suze Weinberg* Ultra Thick Embossing Enamel • *JudiKins* Diamond Glaze • Gold leaf • *Duo* Adhesive
1. Paint the spine of book with Walnut ink. Splatter the front and back covers with Walnut Ink as well and let dry. **2.** Smear *Lumiere* Gold paint on covers. **3.** Stamp Bamboo stamp with *Ancient Page* Black ink across book covers. Let dry. **4.** Stamp Fern with *Lumiere* Gold paint. Be sure to wash stamps immediately after use with *Lumiere*. Let book dry. **5.** Stamp Ancient Artifacts in *Ancient Page* Sienna ink. Cover completely with Ultra Thick Embossing Enamel and heat until melted and molten. Crack. Glue to book with Diamond Glaze. **6.** Attach spine cover with *Duo* adhesive. Let set. Add variegated gold leaf.

Creating... On the Edge

Don't overlook the edges of your pages.

This is a natural place to add a bit of excitement or finishing touch to an altered book. Your altered book should be pretty much finished by the time you finish the edges or paint will mar the edges as you work and you could accidentally make a mistake on your edge while working on another page.

You can use anything from regular pigment inks and fluid chalks to a marker to glazes and fluid acrylics on the page edges. Be sure to flip the pages open while the drying process is going on to prevent sticking. Also use a dry brush if painting with fluid acrylics.

1. Clip text block together with bull dog clips.

2. Do 'direct to paper' with fluid chalk inks to paper edges. Move clips as you work.

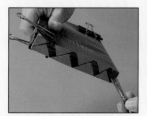

3. Paint any abstract design you choose with fluid acrylics and a flat brush (*Loew-Cornell* Comfort 3300 shader #10). Flip the pages as they dry.

4. Use a silver metallic brush pen to add accents.

Book One: Spiral

With a damp cloth, pick up a small amount of *Golden* glaze colors. Sponge across the book edges. Do all painting with *Golden* fluid acrylics. Draw squiggles with Black and White markers.

Book Two: Checks

Make a checkerboard using *Krylon* markers in Gold and Copper. Let dry. Place a small dot using Silver in each gold square to finish the look.

Book Three: Betsy's Flowers

With a damp cloth, pick up a small amount of *Golden* glaze in Burnt Sienna. Sponge across the book edges. Do all painting with *Golden* fluid acrylics. Lines were worked in Quinacridone Burnt Orange. Paint leaves with Yellow Oxide mixed with a touch of Carbon Black. Shade flowers and leaves with Raw Umber and highlight with Titan-Buff.

Book Four: Zigging and Zagging

Do 'direct to paper' with *ColorBox Cat's Eye* Blue fluid chalk ink. Let dry. With a *Loew-Cornell* Comfort 3300 shader #10, paint a zigzag border with *Golden* Bone Black fluid acrylic. Use a small amount of paint on your brush. Do one side at a time and flip through the pages as the paint dries. Finish by accenting with a Silver metallic brush marker.

Grids and Squares

An easy composition style is a grid.
The following pages show the grid as seen by a couple different artists. You can easily do a grid and then break the mold by laying another image over part of the grid.

What is Composition and why should I care about it?

In a collage, how the elements arranged on a page is the composition. Most people work in a portrait composition. This means that the focal point is smack dab in the center of the page.

This is an easy composition, but by no means the only one. Most compositions are arrived at through an organic process, but you can reverse this process and pick a composition to try. It is an interesting exercise and a good way to wake up your brain.

The facing page showcases one kind of composition... the grid as seen by two different artists. Though their styles differ, the composition is similar.

How would you interpret this composition?

Sky-Blue
by Chris Vietmeier

This double spread has a curved and intersecting composition. The striped collage elements bring your eye around the pages while the curves direct your eye as well. A Coptic marker airbrush and old doily make an interesting background.

MATERIALS: Collage papers • Coptic marker airbrush system • *Coptic* Blue markers • *Uhu* glue sticks • Ruler • Craft knife
1. Take an old plastic doily and lay it on the page. Use an airbrush to color the background in blues. Pick up the doily and let it dry. 2. Use collage paper and continue with the blue theme. Cut squares and strips to help your eye move around the page.

Emerson
by Nancy Curry

This grid is made of collage material that came entirely from one catalog.

The patterns really jump out due to the black and white color scheme.

MATERIALS: 1" square punch • Gesso • Paintbrush • *Uhu* glue stick • Catalogs, junk mail and magazines • *Yasutomo* White gel pen • White paper • Black paper • Painter's tape • Black acrylic paint • Correction tape

1. Prep book with gesso to whiten the background. **2.** For a composition strong in contrast, punch 12 squares out of your catalogs. Use primarily black and white images, intermixing a few with hints of color. **3.** Affix squares to White paper, then Black paper. **4.** Handwrite an Emerson quote around the squares with a White gel pen. Affix to dry book. **5.** Facing Page: Carry Gesso out from the spine using painter's tape as a border. Use correction tape to block out specific words. Paint page with Black acrylic paint. Pull tape off when dry to reveal words.

Mail Art Book
by Erika Tysse

This grid theme has been taken to the extreme with the use of art stamps that accent the theme. Each grid is worked as a small piece of wonderful art.

MATERIALS: Art stamp grid papers • *Artchix Studio* Tracyroos image • *Fusion Art Stamps* stamps • Collage papers including, handwritten letters, train tickets, vintage cards, found photos, grid paper • Brads • Red paper • Sandpaper • Gesso • *Golden* Gel Medium • Velvet ribbon

1. Lightly sand your board book so paint and glue will adhere.

2. Collage a sheet of small artist stamps on perforated art stamp paper. Treat each stamp as a mini work and use red as a theme.

3. Attach stamped sheet to Red paper with brads **4.** Glue entire page down to a board book. Add a velvet ribbon to the center of page.

Sewing in Altered Books

I love the sewn look in collage work. To sew in your book you need to handstitch or sew the collaged pieces with the page out of the book and then glue it in. I have sewn on a folded page before and managed to get the book in my machine. Play around with different stitches. Zig zag and decorative stitches on your machine add a fun element. I enjoy handstitching as well and have learned to use Kreinik paper needles when stitching. The shape of the needle helps the holes in the paper.

Tag Page   by Erika Tysse

Collaged tags are sewn by machine. The zigzag stitch gives the page extra zip and romance.

MATERIALS: Shipping tags • Paper bag • Fibers • Charms • Vintage images
1. Glue down part of a paper bag. **2.** Collage vintage papers and found items to shipping tags. **3.** Add fibers and charms to tags **4.** Sew down tags with thread and a sewing machine. **5.** Glue in book.
Tip: These images where actually done in a vintage photo album. It was taken apart to work on.

Photographic   by Erika Tysse

MATERIALS: Collage elements • Old photos • Vellum • Threads
1. Cut collage materials and photos into 1" squares. **2.** Sew squares to the page. **3.** Add a vellum overlay with the word 'Photographic'

Sewn Collage   by Randy Keenan

This modern collage was sewn together with a sewing machine then glued into a book. I like the modern crisp edges. The paste paper almost looks like fabric

MATERIALS: Paste Paper • Sewing machine • Music • Collage papers
1. Cut extra paste papers in geometric shapes. **2.** Tear some sheet music paper. **3.** Lay out papers in a pleasing way and lightly glue together. **4.** Sew on machine following some lines. **5.** Glue into book.

Bessie
by Beth Cote

This book is dedicated to my great grandmother who I never met, but feel like I know from the wonderful stories my grandmother shared. The found objects in the niches are a reflection of her.

It is part of a series of gallery work I did in 2002/2003 that are more sculptural books and was shown at the Altered Book Exhibit at Ryder University.

MATERIALS: Silk Chiffon fabric • *Lazertran* paper with an old photo copied to paper according to directions • Photo • Slide • Glass slide • Bobbin, star fish, buttons and found objects • *ColorBox* pigment ink (Amber, Ochre, Burnt Sienna) • *Golden* gel medium • Mulberry paper • Sewing machine
1. Glue book open. Rub gel medium into edges of book as if gluing for a niche but leave book open while drying. **2.** Cut three shallow niches. **3.** Do 'direct to paper' over pages. Start with the lightest color and work to the darkest. Add Burnt Copper to edges. **4.** Glue 3D items into niches with gel medium and let dry. **5.** Color copy old photo to Lazertran per directions. Iron it to silk chiffon per directions on package.
6. Cut chiffon to size around book. Use pins and pin together with the book inside. Sew around edges on a machine so they are rough. Rip hole in chiffon. Carefully burn the edges of the chiffon with fire starter.

Chiffon Covering

1. Cut a hole for window, then rip the edges. **2.** Thread your machine needle with Metallic Thread (I used *Kreinik* thread 1700 Misty Gold). Do not knot off thread. Begin with a small running stitch. From the back criss-cross the window and make another running stitch. Continue to do this until the window is as full as you like and the running stitch is all the way around the window. **3.** Secure both ends of thread by gluing a small piece of mulberry paper over thread and collaging over that.

Gypsy Ribbons
by Beth Cote

The whimsy of the gypsy and this page are doubled by the string of eyelets that run down the page like a corset. The only color comes from the vintage tarot card papers and the ribbon running through the eyelets.

MATERIALS: $^3/16$" brass eyelets • *American Tag* extended reach eyelet setter and punch • Collage materials • Vintage tarot card paper • *Artchix Studio* Gypsy • Ribbon

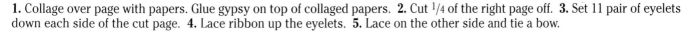

1. Collage over page with papers. Glue gypsy on top of collaged papers. **2.** Cut $^1/4$ of the right page off. **3.** Set 11 pair of eyelets down each side of the cut page. **4.** Lace ribbon up the eyelets. **5.** Lace on the other side and tie a bow.

Butterflies are Jewels by Joy Bathie

In this fairy fantasy page, a butterfly sits in the corner while jewels glitter across the page and leaves sparkle.

MATERIALS: Acrylic paint (Green, White) • Bridal tulle fabric • Heavy Modeling Paste • Beads and other elements • *Golden* gel medium • Gesso • Cast paper butterfly with wire antenna
1. Paint tulle green and let dry. Cut several leaves out of tulle. **2.** Cast a butterfly out of paper and add wire antenna **3.** Gesso pages and paint. Parts of images from the book show slightly through the paint. **4.** Cut a window through two pages with a Craft knife and inset tulle. Glue pages together.
5. Apply modeling paste around window. While wet, texture it with fingers and tools. Stamp textures into the paste. Set in jewels and beads. Let dry. Paint when dry with acrylic paints. **6.** Glue tulle leaves across the pages. Glue butterfly to page.

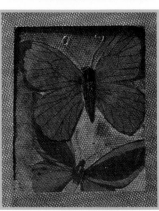

BUTTERFLY DETAIL

TEXTURE DETAIL

CAST BUTTERFLY DETAIL

Using Hard Molding Paste

1. Apply liberal amount of molding paste with plastic spoon; while wet, create curves and niches with fingers. **2.** While wet, press in beads and jewels. All beads, mirrors, and jewels we used are from JewelCraft. **3.** When dry, accent molding paste with paints; Golden Iridescent paint in Pearl.

A Clock for Anna

by Mark Frnka

This clock follows the instructions from Altered Book 101 with Mark's unique vision.

Computer generate numbers and lightly stamp with a texture stamp from *Raindrops on Roses*. Punch out of Green cardstock and acetate with a hole punch. Set the numbers in typewriter keys by *Coffee Break Design* and fold the prongs back. Glue to book. Stamp image A-5 from *Stampington* and emboss on a Mica tile from *US ArtQuest*. Back with decorative papers and glue to book.

Perpetual Motion

by Beth Cote

The deep blues of this page tend to reflect the mood of the main focal point. She seems to be deep in thought and the color shades her pensive mood to a darker mode.

MATERIALS: Hand decorated paper • Black mulberry paper • *Golden* fluid acrylics in different shades of Blues • Transparency of Oxford Impression Stamps • Found collage items • *Postmodern Design* background stamps (Fuzzy numbers, Word slabs) • Screening • *Lumiere* Gold paint • *Uhu* glue Stick
1. Collage papers over page. Glue focal point in place and cover the cut edges to blend. **2.** Stamp background stamps in *Memories* Black. **3.** Paint with fluid acrylics in various shades of Blue. Dab with a damp paper towel, picking up colors that are too strong or cover the images too much. **4.** Glue Black mulberry papers over images. **5.** Paint through a confetti screen with *Lumiere* Gold paint for a textured effect.

Men and Boys

by Wendy Vecchi

Stamped letters are highlighted by the fun use of different fonts and alphabet beads that are sewn into a little window.

MATERIALS: *The Beadery* Alphabet Beads • *Limited Edition* Typewriter key alphabet • *Stampington* Men and Boys stamps • Printed tissue • Stipple brush • *Ancient Page* inks (Browns and Blacks) • Cardstock
1. String beads on Black thread and glue to page over black screen. Glue transparent tissue over pages with windows and cut out where stringed beads sit. **2.** Glue found numbers, stamped and cut typewriter words across the page. Stamp more numbers and words on pages. **3.** Stamp images on cardstock and mat with Black cardstock. Glue to pages. Stipple Brown inks around the edges to age the pages.

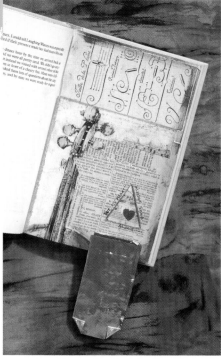

Open the tag door to reveal a niche

Metal will add surprise and luster to your pages like nothing else.

Played the Violin

by Beth Cote

This is a fun double spread. The metal door opens to reveal a small triangle niche and a heart.

MATERIALS: *Autumn Leaves* Paper Violin Concerto • *JudiKins* Quill Flourishes #25901 stamped image • Text paper • *AMACO* Aluminum art foil for art embossing • Copper self-stick tape • Cardstock folded in half with the top half cut like a tag • *AMACO Rub 'n Buff* • *AMACO* Metal Tool

1. Prepare cardstock by scoring and folding it in half. Wrap the upper part in Aluminum art foil. 2. Glue three pages together. 3. Glue a metal door tag to your page with a glue stick. The cardstock part is glued to the page so the metal part opens and shuts. 4. Collage over the page and the cardstock to cover it. 5. Cut a hole behind the door through the cardstock and pages. 6. Outline the hole with a Silver pen 7. Score into the metal with a tool. 8. Rub metal with *Rub 'n Buff*. Let sit for a couple of minutes. Wipe with a paper towel. 9. Accent page with more *Rub 'n Buff*. Be careful; this is strong stuff. Use a small amount. 10. Glue backing to the hole and collage.

Making a Metal Door

1. Cut a piece of cardstock 8" x 2". Fold and score in half. Trim edges for a tag look. 2. Cut a piece of metal 4" x 4". Fold it in half over the top of cardstock. 3. Fold down corners for a tag look 4. Use a hammer and metal stamps to impress a quote into metal.

5. Handpress metal stamps into metal tape to spell a word. 6. Attach Copper tape. You may give the Copper tape a patina with a flame. 7. Roll tape flat with rolling pin or dowel stick. Rub Raw Umber glaze into metal creases and words. Let dry.

Using Metal in Your Altered Books

I love the metal look in altered books. I was tempted to metal by a great altered book artist, Karen Michel.

She showed me something called high temperature flume tape that construction workers use to patch duct work. It looks like ordinary metal but has a great adhesive on it and can be wrinkled and torn.

I figured out that you can use metal stamps and just press them into the tape instead of using a hammer. You can also use Copper tapes and gold tapes and press words into them. Tape them up and you have patchwork.

Think of the possibilities.

X-Ray of My Hand   by Beth Cote

I designed this window around a very cool tag I received in an alphabet tag swap that was hosted by Teri Bollinger.

The tag was designed on acetate with a heart in the x-ray. The fantastic artist gave me permission to use her art in this project and the metal rimmed window is the result.

MATERIALS:
- Flume Tape
- Metal alphabet stamps
- Collage material
- White and Black gesso
- Sandpaper
- *Lumiere* Gold paint

1. Glue two pages together. Cut a hole in the middle of the pages.
2. Collage around the page.
3. Wipe gesso over collage. Sand a little bit to lift the gesso.
4. Collage more papers. Sand again.
5. Rub a little Black gesso and *Lumiere* Gold paint in places on the collage.
6. Sand again. Wipe a thin coat of White gesso over collage again.
7. Cut a piece of flume tape and push the alphabet stamps into the tape to spell out your message.
8. Rip the message into pieces and place message around the window. Fold the tape over the window as well.

Zines

A great resource for altered books and other mixed media techniques is the world of zines. Zines are small limited edition magazines that are produced usually by one or two people.

They are mostly black and white, highly imaginative and sometimes include great handouts or materials hidden inside them. Here are a list of some of my favorites with contact information, but know that there are dozens out there!

ARTitude Zine
by Helga Strauss & Suz Simanaitis
117-2017 A Cadboro Bay Road
Victoria, BC V8R5G4 Canada
www.artitudezine.com

dog eared magazine
published by Kerrie Carbary
P. O. Box 17545, Seattle, WA 98127
www.dogearedmagazine.com

Feed the Addict
published by Donna Engstrom
c/o The Creative Side
1011 E. Grand River Ave.
Brighton MI 48116
www.thecreativeside.com

The Gleaner
by Sherylynne Carriveau
PO Box 8429, Long Beach, CA 90808
TheGleaner@aol.com

In(ner) question
published by Eliza Badurina
112 So. 9th St., Norfolk, NE 68701
www.moderngypsy.com

Play
by Alternative Arts Products
Tracey and Teesha Moore
Box 3329, Renton, WA 98056
www.teeshamoore.com

Trumpetvine Travels
published by Martha McEvoy
P.O. Box 7935, Berkeley, CA 94707
www.trumpetvine.com

Stuck on Zines and want to know more?? For a complete list look at:

Zine of Zines
by Sherylynne Carriveau
PO Box 8429, Long Beach, CA 90808
TheGleaner@aol.com

On Top of Eyelets:

The best storage:

I like to store my eyelets in a metal watch part container that has small round cans with windows in the lids. You can find them cheap at a great catalog and online shop called www.leevalley.com.

Some Definitions:

Eyelet: An eyelet is the small metal form that has a round lip and a tube, used for attachment.

Grommet: A grommet is the same as an eyelet except larger and used in the fashion industry.

Rivet: This has a flat head, no hole and is used to connect things, especially metal.

Nailhead: This is a decorative element that sits on the paper with prongs instead of having a hole punched.

Why are some eyelets easier to set than others?

If you are using the same setter and notice one kind of eyelet is easier to set than another, it is because of the material the eyelet or rivet is made from. Some eyelets are made of aluminum; others brass, which can be really hard to set.

What is a long eyelet?

A long eyelet is an eyelet that has a long shaft to connect or go through thicker objects or papers like book board.

The perfect eyelet setter?

I love the *American Tag* long reach home pro. I can set any eyelet, rivet or nailhead with one machine and it punches straight through metal and book covers if needed. This machine is heavy and made of metal. It won't wear out in my lifetime and since it is large, I don't misplace it on my work bench.

Nailhead Cover - Siblings
by Beth Cote

The combination of rusty wallpaper, metal nailheads, and vintage beadwork from a ball gown combine for a truly romantic old look for the cover of this book. Though only four main elements are used, the cover appears visually complicated

MATERIALS: Text paper • *Golden* glaze (Violet Earth, Raw Umber) • *American Tag* Nailheads and Nailhead setter • *Lee Valley* Metal file plate • Piece of textured wallpaper that has been "rusted" using *Modern Options* Rust Systems according to directions • *ArtChix Studio* Transparency • Vintage Beadwork • Tacky Glue • Double-sided tape
1. Sponge glazes over an old book with complementary colors to accent and age the cover. I used Raw Umber and Violet Earth. Let dry. 2. Glue text to book cover and glaze to age the text. 3. Rip rusty wallpaper and glue over text. 4. Cut a transparency to fit the plate and use double-sided tape to attach it to metal plate. Back with text so it faces and the transparency shows up. 5. Add double-sided tape to the back of plate and attach to cover. 6. Use tacky glue to adhere the beadwork to cover. 7. Attach nailheads using nailhead setter between beadwork to marry beadwork to book. Fold back spokes with pliers and glue little nailheads to the plate with tacky glue.

Metal Window - Dramatic Faux Metal Background
by Sally Turlington

Real etched, oxidized and discolored metal make this book unique. Everyone will want to know, "How in the world do you get that look?"

MATERIALS: White glue • Candle • Soft rag • *AMACO* Metallic *Rub 'n Buff* • *Golden* fluid acrylics (Quinacridone Gold) • *Golden* regular gel matte • Netting and floral mesh • Thin cardboard • Metal flashing • Copper sheet • Copper mesh • Brads • Staples • Clock face • Miniature knife, amber jewel and other 3D embellishments • *Bond 527* Multi-Purpose Cement or *E6000* • *Radio Shack* PCB Etchant Solution (Silver Black or other oxidizing solution) • *Dover* Copyright-free image • Transparency Sheet

Use waxed paper under the page to protect the rest of the book.

Add the Soot Area - Cover the entire page with a layer of White glue. Before the glue dries, hold the page directly over a lighted candle to cause soot to form over the whole page. Keep moving the book over the candle to avoid burning the page and allow the flame to dry the glue. Keep a wet rag and bowl of water handy in case of fire. This process should be done outside or in a well-ventilated area, as the smoke will be strong. Use a soft rag to wipe soot off the page. If there are areas that are still wet, put the page back over the flame to dry it. Use the rag to briskly rub the dry page. This will polish it and the page will begin to look like dark metal. Use *Rub 'n Buff* to highlight the page with metallic colors. If the page burns through at some spot, glue a jewel or other 3D piece in the hole on the underlying pages to show through the burned hole. Use the same sooted glue method on a small cardboard square and brad it to the page. Add 3D embellishments.

For the facing page, put the flashing in a plastic bag with etchant and leave it overnight. Rinse with water. Discolor the Copper mesh with oxidizing solution. Paint the page with thinly applied fluid acrylic. Cut mesh and netting to fit the page and adhere with gel medium. Adhere the floral mesh over the whole page and adhere the two layers of netting only on the edges to allow slight movement. Layer the Copper mesh and Copper sheet. Cut through both, folding back the edges on top of each other to create a window. Copy the image onto a transparency and glue it to the back of the Copper sheet so it will show through the window. Layer this onto the etched flashing and brad together onto the page. Staple a second etched metal piece or other 3D element below the main windowed piece.

Membrane Transfers

These transfers create a thin see-thru layer of the paper's surface, so images are still recognizable but the background shows through. All variations of this technique involve rubbing off the paper backing and leaving the ink attached to the membrane. There are three different kinds of membrane transfers.

Gold Ring by Beth Cote

The romance and other-worldness of this page is attributed to the 'Tape Transfer'. ColorBox Cat's Eye inks bring in a mist of color and tissue paper from my favorite clothing store finish the effect. Keep your eyes open. You never know where you will find collage materials!

MATERIALS: *Peel n Stick* in Matte • Tissue paper • *Magic Scraps* mosaic tiles in autumn • *Nunn Design* frame • *ColorBox Cat's Eye* (Amber, Moss Green, Roussillain) • Magazine pages
1. Use the *Peel n Stick* and the magazine pages, to make a 'Tape Transfer' (see page 43). I used three different transfers on this page. One is the background, one is the picture of a woman and one is the words. 2. Apply the transfer to your book. Crease transfer if it is going over the gutter. You may need to glue the transfer on the page if the adhesive is worn off. Use a glue stick or gel medium. 3. Apply *Cat's Eye* ink in the 'direct to paper' manner, starting with the lightest color. 4. Apply glue to page and lay tissue down on top of glue. 5. Add color accents with *Cat's Eye* ink. 6. Glue frame and mosaic tiles to page with Gel medium or Ultimate glue.

Forget the Rules by Joy Bathie

The bright color scheme of these pages is accented with a gold thread that is woven around the windows. The color scheme resembles a bright jeweled crown.

MATERIALS: *Golden* fluid acrylic paints • Gold thread • Needle • *Memories* Black ink • *Stampers Anonymous* stamps (Man is a fallen god, Art) • Various letter and number stamps

1. Rip two middle pages out so about 1/4 of the pages are left. Paint the background with acrylic paints so images show through a bit. Paint the middle pages Green and glue to background pages. 2. Rip various holes in pages. 3. Punch other holes. 4. Thread a needle and sew around holes and weave your thread across the window as well. 5. Stamp 'Man is a Fallen God' and 'Art' with *Memories* black ink.

Tape Transfer
also called Cold Laminate, Packing Tape or Contact Transfer

'Tape Transfer' is a very easy transfer. It is the only transfer that will allow you to read the words on the transfer as they appear before the transfer. Another advantage is that you can use magazine images, without color copying them, and you can color the back of the transfer with PearlEx mixed with Diamond Glaze, Metallic Rub-Ons, gold leaf, Marvy metallic markers, etc.

*Most **TAPE** will work for this project... packing tape, clear contact paper, Keep a Memory™ acid-free laminate or Peel n Stick™. The major differences are the thickness or the sheen of the tape (matte or gloss).*

A few drawbacks to different types of tape can be the shiny surfaces of laminate or packing tape and the thick edges which appear around the images because the membrane is thick. The shiny surface can be circumvented by using clear matte tape.

Didn't rub all paper off

Air bubble in Tape

Rub too much

1. Apply **TAPE** over image. If using *Peel n Stick*, cut to size, peel off back, and stick over image. **2.** If using packing tape, zig-zag tape over image and itself to cover everything completely. **3.** Soak in warm water for ten minutes. **4.** Rub back of the image (the excess paper) off with your fingers. It will roll off. **5.** If you want, you can rub Metallic Rub-Ons or *PearlEx* from *US ArtQuest* behind the image for a different effect. **6.** You have a finished transfer.

Tape folded into a crease

Medium Transfers

An old art school image transfer technique is called the matte medium transfer. It has the advantage of being a thinner membrane then the 'Tape Transfer', but it is time consuming.

1. Paint a layer of **GLOSS MEDIUM** (*Golden* Polymer Medium is a good brand) over the image you wish to transfer. Let dry and repeat five times. Let dry overnight. **2.** Let sit in water for 15 minutes **3.** With cheesecloth or a sponge, gently rub away paper off the back of the membrane, just leaving the dried medium. Carefully expose the picture and continue to rub until you get the desired effect. **4.** Adhere to your artwork with more medium.

A variation of this technique is to use one coat of Seal-All Caulk to make a transfer.

1. Apply **SEAL-ALL CAULK** (*Elmer's* is a good brand) to the front of the image and use it like a glue to adhere it to your work. Let dry overnight. **2.** With wet cheesecloth or a sponge, gently rub away the paper off the back of the membrane while it is attached to your work. Carefully expose the picture and continue to rub until you get the desired effect.

Another variation from Becca Krahula is to use three coats of Omni Gel as a transfer.

1. Apply 3 coats of **OMNI GEL** (*Houston Arts* is a good brand) to the surface of an inkjet copy with a brush or a sponge brush, each coat going a different direction. Allow gel to dry 20 minutes between coats and 2 hours when finished. Place in warm water to soak the paper, lay flat on a table then roll off paper in a circular pattern. Apply *Omni Gel* to the back, then press in place.

Image Transfers

An image transfer is lifting an image from one piece of paper and transferring it to another place or another piece of paper. Image transfers are a fun, innovative, and easy way to expand your image catalog without buying lots of stamps.

There are two types of transfers... membrane and chemical. Both have practical sides and uses, so it is important to learn what effect these different techniques have and which will give you the effect you want.

Blue Lady
by Beth Cote

If you have room to make a mistake in a book, feel free to do a transfer inside the book itself. It is always a gamble doing a transfer, so, if you are tight on space, forego this idea. You can always do it outside the book and glue it in.

MATERIALS: Ink jet Printer (home printers by HP, Canon, etc. There are cartridges in an ink jet printer. The printing will smear when wet. If you have one of the new Epson printers that use waterproof ink this will not work).
• Simon or Labelon Image Flow Pro Paper • Light Blue mulberry paper • US ArtQuest *Duo* Glue • *US ArtQuest* Variegated Gold Leaf • *Golden* Indigo glaze • Highly texturized handmade paper • *Golden* Regular Gel Matte
1. Print an image on Image Flow Pro paper using your ink jet printer. **2.** With your finger, smear the Regular Gel Matte directly on the page of your book. **3.** Flip the image so it touches the gel. Quickly burnish the page with a spoon. **4.** Let dry. **5.** Use a sponge and lightly add Indigo glaze to color the edges of the transfer and page. Dab glaze onto the textured paper to color it Blue. Rip the paper into pieces. **6.** Add mulberry paper and textured paper to the edges of transfer. **7.** Brush *Duo* glue on the edges of transfer as well and let dry as directed. **8.** Add gold leaf and brush off excess. Sand over if it is too bright and thick.

Ink jet Transfer with Matte Gel

1. This transfer method depends on the right kind of paper and gel. Use **IMAGE FLOW PRO INK JET PAPER** (*Simon* or *Labeltron* are good brands) and **REGULAR GEL MATTE** (*Golden* is a good brand). **2.** Apply gel to page with your finger. You need a thin coat. **3.** Turn the ink jet print over so the image kisses the gel. **4.** Rub and burnish with a plastic spoon. Work fast and cover all the image. Double burnish face. Lift a corner to see if it transferred. **5.** See finished transfer.

Tip: The only real problem is rubbing too hard. This takes a gentle hand.

Problems

Not burnished enough and missed areas   Too much gel   Laid gel on streaky

Variations

Gel transfer on Legacy Collage Papers   Gel Transfer on Tag

The Chemical Transfer process is as follows:

1. Cut out image to be used. When choosing an image, be aware that words will transfer backwards. Either have them printed as a mirror image or avoid them. **2.** Put the image face down on the artwork. Gently dab acetone or another chemical over the back of the paper. Work fast as the chemical may evaporate quickly. **3.** Burnish or rub the back of the image with a spoon or bone folder. **4.** Peek underneath the page to see if image is transferring. Continue to rub as needed.

Variations - Chemical Transfer

1. Apply Chartpak marker or another chemical to the back of a color copy while it is face down on your page. **2.** Rub and burnish the back of photo with a bone folder or spoon. **3.** As you can see, the transfer is not very clear. This works better on black and white toner copies that are fresh. This is meant to be a ghost-like image

Chemical Transfers

A Chemical Transfer is like those old-fashioned tattoos you would get on the wrapper of a stick of gum. You'd lick the tattoo and slap it on your skin. Hold tight for a couple of minutes and presto! A slightly blurry tattoo. In the transfer process, the chemical you use reactivates the toner in your photocopy or color copy. You burnish it or rub hard and presto! An image, albeit a slightly blurry image.

The following chemicals can be used in this technique, but beware, many are extremely potent and may harm you..

Products for Chemical Transfers:

1. Chartpak marker
2. Xylene is the same chemical in Chartpak markers
3. Acetone or acetone nail polish
4. Wintergreen oil
5. Citra Cell cleaner
6. For ink jet prints: Marvy Magical cleaner

This process will give you a slightly blurred image.
If this process doesn't work here are some possible fixes:

1. Use new copies so the toner is fresh. When copying clip-art or materials, place paper in a zipper bag to decrease the toner evaporation.
2. Some papers have a finish that will not take a transfer. Avoid tightly woven papers or papers with a texture.
3. Some copy machines do not have a lot of carbon in the toner, so the picture will not transfer evenly. *Kinko's* and *Office Max* machines will work, but some workplace machines may use a different ink.
4. Color copies that are very light or have large white areas transfer badly. Choose pictures that have great contrast.

Matte Gel Medium can be used as a chemical agent and as a transfer agent for ink jet prints.

Membrane Transfers

The best way to transfer images for me is using a technique Jonathan Talbot created. This process blends the medium transfer with an iron to create a seamless transfer.

To do this at home you need release paper, a tack iron, and it helps to use transfer paper which is coated with clay and dissolves easily.

All of these supplies can be purchased from Jonathan Talbot on his website at www.talbot1.com

1. Apply one coat of **GLOSS MEDIUM** (*Golden* Polymer Medium is a good brand) over image. This must be even. If it is streaky, you will have white bits on your transfer. Let dry. **2.** Apply one coat of Gloss Medium on the area of your work where the transfer will be placed. **3.** Iron the picture, image side down, onto your art work. **4.** With wet cheesecloth or a sponge gently rub paper off the back of the membrane while it is attached to your work. Carefully expose the picture and continue to rub until you get the desired effect.

Waiting
by Beth Cote

A polymer transfer gives a very crisp image. It is also identical to the original, except it will be mirrored. If you are using a piece of text, have the color copy center make a reverse image.

MATERIALS: Transfer of woman made with Gloss Medium (*Golden* Polymer Medium is a good brand) • Black mulberry paper • *Kreinik* Japanese thread #5 Gold • Collage materials • *Gizmo* Color Cutter or Black marker • Craft knife • *Golden* Red Oxide fluid acrylic • *Lumiere by Jacquard* Sunset Gold

1. Make a polymer transfer. **2.** Glue your images and the transfer to the pages. **3.** Add accents with Black mulberry paper. **4.** Blend the edges of the collage and the sharp corners with the Red Oxide fluid acrylic. **5.** Sponge *Lumiere* Sunset Gold over the collage to continue blending. **6.** Place your cutting mat behind three pages. Use the color cutter to cut through the collage and the pages behind in an organic shape. **7.** Glue the three pages behind the collage together. Hole punch the edges.
8. Thread the Gold thread through the holes. Glue the thread to page with a piece of mulberry paper over the ends. **9.** Cut the piece of collage down a bit following the lines of the hole and slip through the threads.

Gloss Polymer Medium Transfer

1. Apply Gloss Medium (*Golden* Polymer Medium is a good brand) to both image and page that image will be transferred on. Move the brush left to right to apply gloss. **2.** Apply a second coat of Gloss Medium from top of page to bottom. **3.** Iron photo to page with Gloss Mediums kissing. Use release or Teflon paper to protect iron and project. **4.** Dampen back of photo and rub paper off with cheesecloth and fingers.

Variations to Alter the Transfer:
1. Stamp on a Library Pocket and transfer image.
2. Apply *Golden* glaze in Metallic Gold over image to get a different look.
3. Apply transfer onto *Legacy Collage* papers

Problem Solving

1. Thin White streaks indicate you didn't apply an even coat.
2. Holes in the picture indicate that either you didn't iron it together and get a good seal or you are rubbing too hard.
3. The image is hard to see indicates that there is not enough contrast between the image and your background. Either your background is too bright and the transfer is blending in or the image is too light.

Problems

Did not rub enough.   Rub through image

Forgot the 2nd coat of polymer   Air pockets when ironing
medium and too streaky

* If you have a slight White coating,
apply Burnt Sienna Glaze over the image.

Round Robin get-together fun in Fort Worth, Texas.

Host a Round Robin

The first thing is to find a point person, someone who is known as the Host or Hostess. An instructor or person connected with a store is a good candidate or it is just as easy to bring a group of friends or guild together. It is great if the hostess knows most of the people participating in the Round Robin, though that is not necessary.

I have participated in many Round Robins and never met the talented people I shared with.

The next thing is to choose a theme. Some Round Robins let everyone choose their own theme and book, or have a broad theme like colors or collections. It is up to each artist to choose a book and the way they will interpret the theme. Some Round Robins declare which book is going to be sent out. I have participated in two Round Robins like that, Women who run with Wolves and Simple Abundance. Some groups decide the theme by author whether it be Carolyn Keene or Sark. Or try an altered calendar Round Robin where people switch every month. The possibilities are endless.

Decide how many players you want and set a limit to the maximum. If you get overrun with people who want to join, you can always set up another circle and have two circles going at the same time. A good group size to start with is 8 - 12.

Set some basic guidelines including the dates and time for switching and how many pages you would like done in each book. You want to put together a sheet with basic contact information on every player. You will need their addresses, phone numbers and work number.

Occasionally, life happens and people cannot meet their obligations. It is important to be able to contact someone if they miss a swap. Also it is important to keep up communication with all members. If someone is out of town on a swap day, let them know they can drop a book off early and pick up their book later that week.

Remember that the object of this is to share and have fun! Everyone is at a different level on their journey and I have found that I have learned as much from beginners as advanced artists. Just remember to respect each other's art and books. Don't compare yourself to others in the circle. The main thing is to enjoy yourself.

Every Round Robin book needs a couple of things. You need to have an artist sign-in page, a copy of the Round Robin rotation with your name clearly highlighted and a page with directions or your vision about the theme of the book.

Folded Triangle Pages

by Beth Cote

Fold a series of triangle pages to make a mini book within a book. Collage the pages and set with eyelets. I love the way bits and pieces of the collage stick out from the triangles.

This is a simple artist sign-in page. A title, some Lumiere Gold and a piece of a collage is all that covers the page

This artist sign-in page has a glassine envelope with a tag inside for each artist to sign and decorate. On the opposite page there is a story that goes with the theme of this gypsy book.

The back of this book holds the addresses of the Round Robin members along with some rules and the book owner's contact information. This is an important part of a Round Robin book. I know of books that have been sent to the wrong circle. Be sure to list the owner's name clearly.

Here is a library pocket that held library due cards. Each artist signed the card.

Signing Your Book

When you send off a book to a Round Robin, your dreams for the book are only images in your head. By making a special sign-in page, you can give a small voice to your vision and let the artists who participated take a bow.

Tracie Miser had each person in this Round Robin group sign a pre-decorated tag.

This sign-in page is one of my favorites. The fact it is a mini-accordion-book in an altered book is one of the great pleasures of this structure. I also like the bleach stamping that covers the accordion with Lumiere paint accents.

MATERIALS: *Magenta* leaf stamp • White toilet paper • Paint Brush • Raffia • *AMACO Rub 'n Buff* • *Golden* fluid acrylics (Iridescent Bronze, Interference Blue, Transparent Red Oxide, Ultramarine) • *Winsor & Newton* Burnt Sienna ink • Baby wipe

Tree of Dreams
continued from below
7. Paint leaves with Gold, Rust and Bronze paints. 8. Choose words for poem and apply *Rub 'n Buff* over them. 9. Wash over pages with *Golden* fluid acrylics in Iridescent Bronze, then do a wash of Interference Blue followed by multiple washes of Iridescent Bronze and again with Interference Blue. Lay a thick layer of Ultramarine and Transparent Red Oxide.
10. Glue natural raffia down and then glue leaves. Touch up with both Bronze, Gold and Rust paints. 11. Spritz with *Winsor & Newton* Burnt Sienna ink.

Make Toilet Paper Castings

Tree of Dreams
by Jen Worden

This wonderful piece has great dimension from an unexpected source... toilet paper. Create a breath-taking page.

1. Lay 3 sheets of 2-ply toilet paper over a deeply embossed rubber stamp or object. 2. Gently drop water onto toilet paper. Use a paintbrush, add water just until damp. 3. Lay a dry baby wipe or kitchen towel over toilet paper and press gently. Remove excess moisture while pressing. If the stamp detail is fine, you may need to use a bone folder or ball point embosser. 4. Remove baby wipe or towel and let the toilet paper dry completely (usually overnight). 5. When dry, peel toilet paper off the stamp. 6. Paint with acrylics and metallics.

Suppliers - Most craft and variety stores carry an excellent assortment of supplies. If you need something special, ask your local store to contact these companies for:

Golden Artist Colors
188 Bell Road
New Berlin, NY 13411
Zhondra Hart 800-959-6543

ColorBox by Clearsnap
800-448-4862

Jacquard Products
distributed by US ArtQuest
US ArtQuest
800-200-7848

Kreinik Mfg. Co.
www.kreinik.com
fibers 800-537-2166

ThermOWeb
adhesive 800-323-0799
www.thermoweb.com

Silver Crow
Po Box 81242
Pittsburgh, PA 15217
www.silvercrowcreations.com

Loew-Cornell
brushes 201-836-7070
www.loew-cornell.com

Artchix Studios
Helga Strauss
250-370-9985 Canada

Turtle Press Studio
206-706-3186

Postmodern Design
stamps 405-321-3176

Renaissance Art stamps
stamps 860-283-9237

Coffee Break Design
317-290-1542
www.coffeebreakdesign.co

Gizmo Enterprises
954-587-6777
www.colorcutter.com

American Tag Co.
800-223-3956

Limited Edition
888-stamp98

Papers by Catherine
papers 712-723-3334

Time to Stamp
stamps 712-723-3334

JudiKins
stamps 310-515-1115

JewelCraft
505 Windsor Dr
Secaucus, NJ
201-223-0804
www.jewelcraft.biz

Hot Potatoes
stamps 615-269-8002

Omni Gel
www.houstonarts.com

Stampsmith
Estelle Smith
www.stampsmith.net
631-547-5922

Beadery
beads 401-539-2432

Raindrops on Roses
919-571-9060

Sheer Heaven
www.cre8it.com
505-466-0270

MANY THANKS to my friends for their wonderful help and ideas!
Kathy McMillan • Jennifer Laughlin
Patty Williams • Marti Wyble • Janie Ray
David & Donna Thomason